30 Days To A New You

A Step-by-Step Guide to Activate Peak Performance!

I0153545

Gregory Griffith

July 2011

The title and trade address of **30 Days To A New You** are trademarks of the author

Quotations from
The 10 Natural Laws of Successful Time and Life Management
Copyright 1994 by Hyrum Smith

Cover Photo: Munoz Studios
Graphic Design: EJ Graphics: Essex James
Editor: Review Queen: Amy Raubenolt

ISBN 978-0-9796565-1-4
© Copyright 2011 Gregory Griffith
Omnigriff Publishing

What people are saying about
Gregory Griffith and *30 Days to a New You*

Mr. Griffith is a captivating Keynote Speaker who delivers an interactive, fast-paced, "Edu-taining" message that brilliantly cross-collateralizes with his reading product. We were fortunate to book him as our guest speaker at the Institute of Business Entrepreneurship Ceremony after the release of his first book *Activate or Stagnate.* As a business educator it is with the highest merit that I recommend this sought-after speaker to any organization. His dynamic, yet candid, style to engage his audience with a focus on self-discovery and self-motivation is clear and inspirational. ***30 Days To A New You*** is a powerful resource tool that illustrates what it takes to incorporate lifestyle management strategies for success in your personal and business life on a daily basis.
Marcia Notkin
Business Educator/Nationally Board Certified Teacher
Hallandale High School

For the past decade I have witnessed Gregory Griffith utilize his skill-sets, innovation and creativity to create a level of competitive distinction for my business. Greg's personal drive to help my company develop a strategic plan for success has proven to be an invaluable asset to our team. Under his direction and leadership our company garnered a #1 Billboard CD single for our flagship artist Rachel Brown. I highly recommend this book to get your team or you firing on all cylinders for increased productivity, peak performance and enhanced personal empowerment.
Israel Charles
President, CEO: The Urban Music Group
Director of Music Technology; Dillard High School

30 Days To A New You enhances one's sense of leadership intuition. It's a step-by-step guide that illustrates how we can develop our strengths, explore the opportunities before us, analyze past successes and discover how to activate our inner winner.
Bridgette Tate
Assistant Principal of Curriculum
Parkway Middle School, Miami, Florida

Gregory Griffith has definitely made an impact and influence in the lives of many. His new book will definitely take readers to their next level. Read it, respond to his principles, and you will be glad you did.
Robert Lemon Author/Speaker/Trainer

There are many motivators out there today, but I believe Gregory Griffith has a unique ability. He gently merges motivation and inspiration into a powerful message in his book *30 Days to a New You.* The book is supposed to be a 30-day self help study, but I found it such an enjoyable read I finished it in just three days. He deserves congratulations on the book and, in bringing to light the power within all of us!

Mona Meretsky, CSEP
President
COMCOR Event and Meeting Production, Inc.
COMCOR Consulting Services, Inc.

The pioneering perfection of Mr. Griffith inextricably changes the landscape of personal empowerment. The ardent zeal and intense participation exerted in his highly anticipated new book, *"30 Days To A New You,"* provides a day-to-day guide that will empower you to exceed expectations, both personally and professionally, and achieve a lifestyle of success!

Jessel Craig
President Fortress Estates/Senior Auditor
Price Waterhouse Coopers

In everyone's life, they meet people for a reason or a season. When I was blessed with the opportunity to meet and hear Gregory Griffith speak, he sincerely impacted me for a season and his material has changed me for a lifetime. As the Division C Governor for Toastmasters International's District 47, I was amazed at Gregory Griffith's level of skill and expertise as a presenter at the Spring International Speech and Table Topics Contest in Fort Lauderdale, Florida. Gregory is definitely destined for continued success to impact the masses! I highly recommend his new book, *30 Days To A New You*

Melody Tapley, DTM
Division C Governor 2009-2010
Toastmasters International

30 Days To A New You is an inspired, introspective, and motivational guide to self-discovery. It is a blueprint for the 'true" synthesis of Mind, Body and Spirit.

Iris McMurray
Educator/Crisis Counselor/Motivational Leader/Orator
Newark Public School District N.J.

To Alyssa!
For every 30 Days that you grow to be the
unique spirit that God made you to be!

You'll be just 3 when you read this,
but I only pray that you'll read it
for the rest of your life
to empower you to be
the best that you desire to be!

Grandpa Loves You!!!

God Bless You!

ACKNOWLEDGMENTS

To God be the glory for the intrinsic insight to bring this project to the masses.

There have been people who have shown up at the right time and the right place to embrace the need to get this project to the masses. Your presence in my life is absolutely not a coincidence at this time in space. Spirit has a way of just making things happen.

I'm grateful to you all!

To my mother and my father: You both have given me my foundation for creativity to develop the paradigm for success. I know it's in the genes! Thank you!

Maru, it's because of your unconditional love, gratitude and relentless support that I'm able to press on to the light at the end. I know I'm blessed because of your presence in my life. Thank you!

Matthew Bennett, from the day I attended your book-marketing seminar, you've been a very positive inspiration and support to advise and counsel me to take this project to the next level. I'll cherish the sessions; review them and your material for a lifetime. Thank you.

Ellen Burton, your work and insight on the final edit was priceless and lifesaving. I send lots of love for the great contacts. You've been in the publishing game for some time. You've sent the right people to do the right thing at the right time. God bless you!

Santiago Masdeu, a great big thank you to you and your team at Factory Printing.

Steve Goodman, I'm grateful for your input. I'm sure it won't be the last time that we collaborate.

Phil Pozin, your second set of eyes has made all the difference in getting the book professionally ready for print. Thanks a million for the formatting and the book cover advice. You truly saw something I couldn't see. Wow! What a blessing! Thanks!

Luis Macias for IFM Design, you've really made me shine with the website design. Thanks a million. Your level of professional attention to my site has made all the difference. I'm grateful.

Michael Pendleton & BPI, Richard Pelzer & Mega Management and Nate Benson, I'm grateful to you for your PR marketing vision as a team.

Essex James, special thanks for your graphic design work. It definitely helped bring the book up to the next level.

Rev. Robert Lemon, the private sessions with you and your spiritual counsel have been priceless. Your professional insights inspired me to take it to the next level.

Victor Antonio, you'll never know how much it meant for you to stop and have the one-hour session with me about the speaking business. Your perspective has always highly impacted my perspective. Truly appreciate you, Man!

To Rev. Kevin Ross, you will be my mentor for life. I'll always value your professional and personal advice. You've truly led by example. May God continue to manifest greatness in your life.

To my entire family for the love and encouragement you gave me to press on against all odds. Thank you all immensely!

To my sons, Gregory, Jr. and Jonathan, I love you! I live to leave my legacy to you!

FOREWORD

When I reminisce about my childhood, I can say that a month was perceived like a never-ending cycle of events that my mother masterminded. I have memories of 30 long days a month of getting up to the kitchen radio or television rushing to meet the demands of my structured school day. The nine months of school were like a journey into the infinite. Then, finally, it was summer!

My perception of my environment created a paradigm shift. Every day was full of infinite opportunities to use my imagination to tap into the intrinsic, inherent, innate, inborn world of creativity. Without doubt, fear, or intimidation, I would climb trees and play games that pushed my physical body to the limit and continuously expand my cognitive domain from the everyday challenges of just finding something new and creative to do. There weren't the multiplicity of options available to a kid in the sixties like we have for our children in our present day and time. I recently watched an evening news segment that quantified my point. The report took a survey of kids who were tech savvy. They were computer literate, owned an iPod and video games of choice. Their parents had Internet access. These kids frequently accessed Google for information.

The hypothesis was created from this question: Are kids now lazy because of technology? Are they less creative? The report seemed to indicate that kids don't have to think. Google does it all. They don't have to be as creative. Their cognitive domains are bombarded with quick access to information with minimal need to exhibit retention or recall. Just log back on to Google! The report ended with a question that creates curiosity. Are kids of the technology age as creative as we were in the sixties?

By now you're probably trying to grasp my analogy to reality. What does this have to do with the title of this book? *30 Days to a New You* is a challenge to take all of your cognitive skills and environmental contacts and utilize them to be a peak performer like the kids of the sixties. Peak performers are creative visionaries. Now that we're adults and our parents aren't the masterminds of our futures, it's a month-to-month, year-to-year challenge to expand the paradigm.

Hyrum W. Smith, the CEO of the Franklin Quest Company who created the Franklin Planner best stated it from his book *The 10 Natural Laws of Successful Time and Life Management*. "The demands of the competitive marketplace put such a premium on personal productivity that if you're not productive, you're out. The result is a tremendous pressure to perform, coupled with an overwhelming insecurity about the future." Mr. Smith subtitled the book: *Proven Strategies for Increased Productivity and Inner Peace*. It wasn't until Hyrum Smith took the 30-day challenge to create his own company that he found success and inner peace as a peak performer.

The *30 Days to A New You* challenge isn't easy, but it is absolutely necessary to find true success and inner peace. Honest, realistic, assessment of where you are from a mental, physical and spiritual perspective is extremely difficult to determine. The obscure chaos of survival often tends to take precedence. We become complacent, maintaining our comfort zones.

Dr. Phil McGraw spoke about our internal dialogues and internal filters in his book *Self Matters*. They establish templates for decision-making that allow us to discern, take action and move forward with a positive attitude.

I have facilitated workshops for diverse groups of people. I'd often ask them a couple of questions to see where their awareness levels were from a cause and effect perspective from a simple five letter word. Very few knew what the word was. When I revealed the answer as HABIT, most in attendance would agree that habits have a powerful cause and effect outcome on successful living. I still find it amazing to see how many people are just living in the box with bad habits that stagnate their ability to be peak performers and true captains of their ships.

My intent with this book is to share personal insights and strategies from my life experiences as a teacher for 20 years, CEO of my corporation since 1992, motivational speaker, author, consultant, 15-time marathon runner and proud father of two sons that will empower you with enhanced peak performance skills to take your life to the next level. *The 30 Days To a New You* challenge is totally up to you to shift the paradigm and create the platform for change and increased productivity; and, as Mr. Hyrum Smith found, discover and maintain lasting inner peace.

May your quest to be the very best manifest from this 30-day test.

Gregory Griffith

Table of Contents

Introduction

*"30 days has September,
April, June and November..."*

It took Noah a little more than thirty days to find dry land.

It took General George B. McClellan thirty days to capture Yorktown during the Civil War.

Morgan Spurlock proved a point by eating only McDonalds for thirty days in "Super Size Me"

And, according to conventional wisdom, it takes thirty days to form a new habit or break an old one.

Are you willing to give thirty days to change your life forever?

If so, read on...

What exactly will the next thirty days bring? The only thing that anyone can say with 100% certainty about the next thirty days is that they will pass. You can just keep doing what you are doing, and time will go by and you will just be thirty days older—or you can use that time to take the first steps in being thirty days closer to living the life of your dreams.

Renowned Motivational Speaker, Gregory Griffith, has pooled his years of experience as a teacher, a marathon runner, a successful musician, and has created a 30-day plan to jump-start your life.

In each of us is an infinite amount of energy to reach our maximum potential. Not realizing that is like keeping the engine running but never stepping on the gas. To drive on the highway to success, you have to give more to be more. I invite you to spend the next thirty days with me learning to shift the gears of your life into overdrive!

I call my 30-day plan to a new you my Personal Empowerment Recognition Program (PERP). PERP is a direct outgrowth of my experiences as an Exceptional Student Education (ESE) teacher. ESE students have learning disabilities that make it difficult for them to process, retain, and recall information. Although I had worked in education as a substitute teacher, taking on ESE classes was my first full-time teaching assignment. As I did with all things in my life, I approached this gig with unbridled enthusiasm—determined to be the very best ESE teacher Coconut Creek High School, in Florida, had ever seen. I could not have foreseen the challenges ahead.

In that first year, although I had six classes of students, I didn't even have a classroom of my own. I had to push a cart loaded down with my materials, hustling to get to each class and to get ready to help kids who didn't even want to be in school. Even when they showed up, I was challenged to get them motivated, focused, and eager to learn.

My ESE classes were larger than usual; and, in addition to their learning disabilities, most of my students were also emotionally handicapped (EH). EH students can be moody and sometimes extremely violent. I knew for me to succeed with these students, I had to develop non-traditional teaching methods to create an environment that would make them want to learn. That's where PERP came in. I created a motivational program based on sharing the richness and empowerment of the written word with my students on a daily basis. Every day when they entered the classroom I would have a motivational journal of inspirational information that I would have them copy into their own composition book.

With these exercises, I learned as much about myself and achieving my own personal best as my students did about themselves. We grew together. Our great discussions and open dialogues helped me create lasting student/teacher relationships with kids who opened their hearts and their minds to me. They left my classes believing they were unique and could make a contribution to society, regardless of the extent of their learning disability. PERP helped each student establish basic foundations for physical, mental and spiritual development. This allowed them to become successful in transitioning to post-secondary school life. PERP gave each student an opportunity to discover his or her purpose and passion for life.

This formed the basis of the PERP program I am about to share with you. If these kids could get over the hurdles life had dealt them and unleash their own "inner winners"—don't you owe it to yourself to spend the next thirty days unlocking your limitless potential too?

You are holding my Greatest Hits, the best of my motivational thoughts and actions. I have compiled thirty of my most effective strategies and inspirational messages from hundreds of the successful PERP sessions I've had over my 20 years as an ESE teacher. I'm presenting these thirty strategies to empower you and your family to take charge of your life and your future.

Why thirty? So this can be a 30-day program to awaken your sleeping dragon. Consider it your 30-day free trial—like the software companies give you to download some new program that will speed up or enhance your computer—before you get the "full" version and amp up your life forever!

The PERP Questionnaire that you will find on the following page and at the conclusion of your 30 Day readings should be read before and after you start and after you have completed the *30 Days To A New You* journey.

In thirty days, I personally guarantee that your life will be improved and different if you honestly answer the questions and get fired up and remain focused about your life.

Get ready to take charge of your life, activate your peak performance skills, and experience enhanced productivity in all areas of your personal and business life NOW! Remember: N.O.W. means No Other Way! Good luck! God Bless you and your family!

Personal Empowerment Recognition Program (PERP)

Questionnaire

Physically

- Are you exhibiting your optimum physical appearance (OPA)?
- Are you disciplined about exercise?
- What are you fueling your tank with?
- Are you aware of the consequences of ignoring the physical?

Mentally

- Are your goals set to achieve greatness with the skills you possess?
- Do you feel you're ready to meet the mental challenge?
- Will fear of failure be the winner?
- Are you a peak performer?
- Are you honestly trying to expand mentally?

Spiritually

- Are you in touch with the Source?
- Have you discovered where the real power is?
- Do you know how important creativity is to your success?
- Are you being unique or trying to blend in?
- Are you utilizing your inner perspective to grow from every external challenge?

In each of us is an infinite amount of
energy to reach our maximum potential.

Not realizing it is like having an *engine running*
but never putting the gear shift in *drive*.

When you awake, you have to *activate the energy* within
by giving more to simply be more.

You've got to *activate* your thoughts to drive
on the highway to success or you'll stagnate
from procrastination. It's your choice.

Activate or Stagnate!
Nothing happens if you don't take action! Don't
procrastinate to the point of stagnation!
Plan your strategy. Stay consistent,
FIRED UP and FOCUSED!

Day 1 - *On Your Mark, Get Set...YOU!*

*"If you don't know where you are going,
you'll end up someplace else."* Yogi Berra

You've heard it all before: *Today is the first day of the rest of your life.* Yes, it's a bit of an overused cliché, but you know something about clichés? There is often a lot of truth to them. It does not matter what it is we are trying to do, what change we are trying to make, what good habit we are trying to start, or what bad habit we are trying to break, getting started is the hardest part.

As we sit there and wrestle with taking that first step towards change, we let ourselves get overwhelmed by the burden of it all. Even with the best of intentions, changing a behavior—doing something differently for the rest of your life—can seem like a Herculean task.

But what if you didn't have to consider doing it for the rest of your life? What if you thought about it as that "free trial" I mentioned earlier, a sample, a temporary change you could make maybe for just the next thirty days. Wouldn't that make taking that first step a little easier? Yes? Good because now you only have 29 more days to go!

In life we often make excuses for why we don't seek to reach our maximum potential. How many times have you had an idea that required a little more of your time and focus to get results? Instead of working to bring your idea to fruition, you ignore that idea and settle more deeply into your comfort zone? You fill your internal dialogue with "I cant's" that become insurmountable obstacles to your growth.

I know because I was a victim of the same circumstance. I worked my job and came home to a routine regimen, until I realized that I deserved more than the comfort and perceived security of an 8 to 5 job. I realized that was only going to make someone else richer and, in the long run, far more secure than I'd ever be.

I'm sure you have a daily routine from which you can't deviate without creating a conflict within your family, girlfriend or boyfriend, manager, or even neighbor. But sometimes you have to be willing to shake it up a bit and take a serious look at where you are. You need to determine if that is really where you want to be in life physically, mentally, and spiritually. The foundations for success in life—to obtain and maintain a balanced lifestyle—lie within those three areas. I asked you to answer the questions from a mind, body and spirit perspective to bring this awareness to the forefront in your life.

Procrastination is the major reason for stagnation of the mind, body and spirit. Don't be a victim of circumstance like I was. I started to eat healthier foods, exercise on a regular basis, and set challenging, realistic goals to advance my position in life, and I consistently seek to grow from the spiritual perspective and from my belief that faith works wonders!

Do You Have a FOUNDATION?

**How *quickly* do we forget that the
tree is supported by its *roots?***

**If you *start* with a good *foundation,*
you will be prepared to handle
life's complex situations.**

**The *balance* we need can only be found
using the right combination of
*physical, mental, and spiritual foundations.***

**Build your *life* like the *roots* of an old tree;
it's the beginning of your own
personal life history.**

Day 2 - Use What You Have

"We are all inventors, each sailing out on a voyage of discovery, guided each by a private chart, of which there is no duplicate. The world is all gates, all opportunities."
Ralph Waldo Emerson

Every journey starts someplace. Even the Universe, as grand and infinite as it may be, had a starting point, a beginning, and a foundation. Webster's defines "foundation" as the groundwork upon which anything is built. In each of us is the foundation we need to succeed. We all have the tools we need to grow physically, mentally, and spiritually. But that combination, that framework, is different for each of us. The point is that to get where you want to be over the next thirty days you need a starting point, but you do not have to reinvent the wheel. *Use what you have*—the talents, the skills, the passions that you have been blessed with, and build a foundation that will become your unique groundwork for success.

When you picture the word foundation, you may think of rigidity—of the strength of the roots of the tallest tree or the bricks and mortar that hold up your home. But that is only one aspect of a foundation for life. The Zen masters say, "A willow's branches may be whirled about by the will of the wind, and yet, its roots remain firm, and the tree unshaken, whereas the mightiest oak is uprooted by the tempest." An oak is known for its strength, size and longevity and a willow for its graceful flexibility. In the face of a violent storm, the ridged oak tree holds its ground, resisting the winds with all of its strength until it finally snaps. The willow, on the other hand, will survive the same storm because of its flexibility by simply flowing with the wind and fury of the storm. You must establish a balanced foundation to accommodate the continuum of life's changes and to weather its storms.

I have two sons, Gregory and Jonathan. Both were given foundations for success at very early ages in different environments and under different parental supervision. Gregory was shifted between parents early and didn't get the attention that his younger brother Jonathan benefited from. Gregory's groundwork was laid before I realized how important balanced foundations are for success.

21

Granted, both my sons are very stable, healthy and intelligent. Gregory struggled more than Jonathan only because I delayed in establishing correct foundations for him. If more parents remember that the tree is supported by its roots, we'll have a more balanced, successful society physically, mentally and spiritually.

The imbalances that exist in our society have a chaotic affect on us all. As a high school teacher and a coach for 20 years, I see the blatant apathy among those who are responsible for establishing the foundations for success. I see our lack of balanced foundations reflected in a country with a 65% obesity rate, a lack of creative finesse, and a moral and spiritual decline that has manifested as a large prison population, lowered numbers of college graduates, and a spiritual struggle amidst a dehumanizing high-tech society.

Don't be a victim of apathy.

Establish the FOUNDATIONS!

Yesterday. Last month. Last year.
All are part of our personal history books. It's good to take a mental look back at them, but please do not get hooked on the events of the past.

Nothing you can do now will change that which simply has passed. It's a new day! You now have the chance to travel life's roads a different way.

To start again is a beautiful part of the next beat of your heart. Get the rhythm of life right---now!
Set new goals.

Don't let fear stop your chance to dance to the rhythm of life.

HAPPY NEW YOU!!!

Day 3 - Keep Your Eye on the Prize

"You can clutch the past so tightly to your chest that it leaves your arms too full to embrace the present."
Jan Glidewell

Okay, it is Day 3 of our 30-day journey, but we both know that more than two days have passed to bring you to this point in your life's overall personal journey. To keep your eye on the prize, it is important to learn from the past, without becoming consumed by it. You cannot see where you are going if you keep looking behind you.

Today, I want you to try something new—anything at all. Meet one new person today. Go to that restaurant you always wanted to try or sign up for that class you have been meaning to take. Stop the excuses and do just one new thing that you have never done or never would have done in the past.

You need to be willing to break the pattern. If you are unhappy about something, change it. All things in the universe are governed by cause and effect. Any given result is preceded by specific action. If you want different results, you have to change the pattern of the preceding action. You cannot expect to lose weight if you keep eating jelly donuts for breakfast every morning. The same goes for getting ahead; you won't achieve your goals until you leave your self-doubts and limits in the past where they belong.

I vividly remember the spring of 1990. I was experiencing a very, very happy new year. My son Jonathan was born on February 27th. His mother had conceived against all the odds. Jonathan was our miracle baby. I was working as a full-time musician six nights a week and as a substitute teacher during the day to support my family.

I'd been performing for about seven months at a nightclub in Ft. Lauderdale, Florida when I got a reminder of the true instability of the entertainment business. I arrived at work as usual and was asked to speak to the club's manager on my break. He informed me that the club was happy with our services, but had an opportunity to book an act that was available only for a few weeks.

We were supposed to be hired by my agent to start another club the next week and return to play at the current club when the road band completed their show. It didn't happen! I was now faced with a dilemma. I have a newborn baby, no job, and my wife was on maternity leave. I'd lost jobs in the past, but never when I had a baby to feed, a mortgage to pay, and two car payments to make each month. I was also my band's leader and manager, which meant I had the financial livelihood of six other musicians on my shoulders. Boy, was it time for me to get the rhythm of life right.

The next day I decided to set new goals for my family and my future. I continued to work as a musician, but I made a commitment to go back to school and get a more secure financial base. I applied for graduate school and found that one class at Barry University in Miami would cost me $500. I applied for financial aid and went to school on Saturdays from 8 am to 5 pm for one year. My last show on Friday nights didn't finish until 3 am. Could you just imagine how I felt on Saturday mornings?

But I made the commitment to not look back at my past. I took a look to learn from it, but didn't get hooked. I had to travel life's road a new way. I graduated one year later, and became a full-time high school teacher and coach.

What is your current dilemma? Do the obstacles seem insurmountable? Are you going to let the fear monster stay on your back and stop you from reassessing your life for the new you? NOW is a powerful three-letter word. I use it as an acronym - **N**o **O**ther **W**ay. **NOW!**

Maybe my little story will get you fired up and focused **NOW** for the new you. Only then will you take charge of your life and reach for the next level.

Life is always about the next level! As they say at Adidas®:

"IMPOSSIBLE IS NOTHING!"

HIT THE HOMERUN!

You are the *umpire* in the game of *life!*

You can go to bat as often as you like
until you hit a homerun!

Strikeouts are never failures.
Each one is just a learning experience
that prepares you to hit the homerun!

Never give up on your dream!
Keep going to bat until you

HIT THE HOMERUN!

Reflections for Remediation, Retention, and Recall . . .

Day 4 - Release Your Fear of Failure

"The only thing we have to fear is fear itself - nameless, unreasoning, unjustified terror which paralyzes needed efforts to convert retreat into advance."
Franklin D. Roosevelt

The Vice President of Columbia films once told a brash and cocky young actor that "he would never make it in this business." His name was Harrison Ford. Walt Disney was fired from his first job with a local newspaper because the editor said he "lacked imagination and had no original ideas." It was Thomas Edison who said, "I never failed, I just found ten thousand ways that didn't work." It is not failure that holds people back. It is the *fear* of failure. The only difference between success and failure is the number of times you get up after you have been knocked down. You only fail when you refuse to get back up again.

Do you think the great Willie Mays hit a homerun the first time he went to bat? We only know about the homeruns. Did you ever stop to think about how many times Willie struck out before he hit that first homerun?

DO YOU REALLY THINK THAT WILLIE MAYS WOULD HAVE EVER HIT A HOMERUN IF HE DIDN'T KEEP GOING TO BAT?

Life will throw quite a few curve balls at you. Just don't be afraid to strike back. The key is to not give up. Stay in the game and keep getting up to bat; sooner or later, you'll make a connection and hit the big one!

No matter how many times Lucy pulled the ball away from him, Charlie Brown kept trying to kick it. No matter how many times the kite-eating tree grabbed his kite, he never gave up; he still got out there and flew it. Eventually "Good Ole Charlie Brown" even got to kiss the Little Red Haired Girl of his dreams! We can all take a life lesson from Charles Schultz's venerable round-headed kid!

Think about the story of Sarah Reinertsen. She had her left leg amputated at birth due to a rare birth defect. At the age of seven, she wanted to play soccer. Her coach took one look and made her just practice kicking the soccer ball against a wall. Through physical therapy and perseverance, she learned how to run with a prosthetic leg and has never looked back! Sarah forgot soccer, but went on to become a world-class sprinter, half and full marathoner for ladies with a prosthesis. She went on to train and compete in triathlons in college. Sarah is presently training to be the first female amputee to finish an iron man triathlon. I am confident she will reach this goal. Sarah actually wanted to quit several times in her career before going on to smash the world record for female above-the-knee amputees.

Sarah never gave up on her dream. Sarah realized that achievement of her dream is always closer than it seems. You have got to think like Sarah! Keep going to bat!!

Just as a tadpole grows to become a frog,
and an acorn becomes a tree,
so should you be able to realize
your full growth potential.

You see, we're all part of a WONDERFUL DIVINE
plan that allows each of us to reach
OUR maximum potential hand in hand.

The only difference between you and the tadpole
is your ability to plant the seeds
for the maximum growth potential
that only you can feed.

Day 5 - Realizing Your Growth Potential

"The only way of finding the limits of the possible is by going beyond them into the impossible."
Arthur C. Clarke

Your ideas are just like the acorn. They're full of all the right ingredients and have unlimited potential to reach fruition. But you must be the driving force. You have to get up every day and feed your ideas and your goals with your relentless and positive energy—just as the sun and rain nurtures that acorn.

Yesterday we discussed getting over your fear of failure, and we pointed out several examples of famous and not-so-famous people who never gave up until they achieved success. They all had three things in common: an unbridled belief in their potential for success and personal growth, a realized need to take action, and practical plans to do so. Belief is a powerful thing, but faith and determination alone are not enough.

Glass ceilings only get in your way when you see them. Barack Obama was not only propelled to the White House by his unwillingness to accept that he did not belong there, but by the way he used that belief to drive his potential and resolve problems. It wasn't enough for him to say that an African American *could* do this; he had a plan and used emerging technologies such as the Internet and social media to turn a traditional political campaign on its ear!

I remember when I was 12 and my older brother Nelson gave me my trumpet. He said something very simple but powerful to me. He said. "You must practice every day to get better. No practice! Stagnation! Frustration!" Well, as a 12-year-old, I had my long moments of frustration and procrastination. But let me tell you this, when I started to practice every day, I got results. I began to play all my scales, and my armature strengthened. I established the foundation for success as a musician. I went on to make my middle school band and played first trumpet. Nelson and I went to Middleton High School in Tampa, Florida where he recently retired from his teaching career. I remained fired up and focused on playing, and made the band there as well. I continued to feed the acorn of the idea that I could be a great trumpet player. But it wasn't only my belief that I could be good that improved my sound; it was practice, practice, practice!

I graduated from high school, and I had the ultimate challenge of making the Florida A&M University Marching Band, as Nelson had. I remember how I would watch him march in the big homecoming parades, and I dreamed of the day I'd be there too. I made the band! After a rigorous training regimen and several challenging auditions, I was chosen from among some 200 of the best musicians who had tried out. I'll never forget the feeling of wearing the uniform for homecoming and feeling like a winner.

I planted the seed. The rest was left up to me. Isn't it time for you to plant some seeds? Maybe you've started to get a degree or high school diploma after many years of procrastination and stagnation. Maybe there's a book you'd like to complete. Maybe there's that great idea for a business that you've just stopped feeding. I could go on and on about the infinite possibilities that could be waiting from something as simple as a focused, committed seed to see the dreams become a reality.

It's never too late to plant a seed.

**New beginnings are sometimes the best thing
that could happen to us.**

Change gives us the chance to start again.

**Remember you always have a choice,
but choices still have consequences.**

If you do nothing, nothing will change.

**Doing something opens the door to
new and unlimited opportunities.**

**Don't let the "fear" of change lead to "stagnation!"
Believe in yourself no matter what others say!**

The unique you will shine through.

Day 6 - Leave Your Comfort Zone

*"Our greatest glory is not in never falling
but in rising every time we fall." Confucius*

Let me ask you a question. Are you happy? Or are you just comfortable? Actually, that was two questions. Here is another: How does a person even measure happiness? Certainly throughout our lives what we think will make us happy changes. At 6, a heavily frosted cupcake was probably enough! As an adult, what is it? A great job, a wonderful relationship, and a trip around the world? Or are we confusing happiness with wants or desires?

Our Founding Fathers knew that happiness is something we all want, but also realized that it is something to be sought after, but not necessarily obtained, as they guaranteed us the right to the *pursuit* of happiness and not the right to the *attainment* of happiness. The dictionary defines pursuit as "an effort to secure or attain; quest." That means to gain happiness takes effort and an ability to leave our comfort zone, embrace change, and not accept the status quo. I believe that finding true happiness is much less about the things we do, the things we have, or even our achievements, than it is about the choices we make. In fact, many believe that happiness itself is a choice. Abraham Lincoln once said, *"Most people are about as happy as they make up their minds to be."* How you view the world and your place in it is a conscious choice—just as it is your choice to stay where you are physically, spiritually, and emotionally or to move on to a better, happier place.

When our comfort zones are threatened, we tend to obscure the possibilities inherent in change. All that matters is *what if I fail? Or what if I can't maintain my basic standard of living*? Security versus freedom and peace of mind becomes the primary issue when we face significant life changes such as considering a career change or divorce. A positive attitude is one of your most important weapons against the fear of change. When your attitude is right, the universe answers your call with the same level of energy that you give to it.

I remember reading the true story from the book, *Attitude Is Everything* by Keith Harrell. Keith was a great All-American high school and college basketball player. His attitude about life was always extremely positive, and Keith had his goals set to become an NBA first-round draft pick right up until the day the NBA draft took place. When that day came and Keith wasn't drafted, he was crestfallen. His attitude toward life took a full reversal, and a downward spiral ensued.

Keith became very pessimistic about his life and eventually obscured all the great possibilities his college degree offered him, even if he didn't become a professional athlete. It wasn't until someone saw him painting houses in Alaska and helped him to see that he had so much more to offer life and himself, beyond being just a basketball player, that Keith changed his attitude and chose to make a change. Using his other strengths, he became a very successful salesman for IBM.

Keith had been so set in his comfort zone with sports that he was terrified to do anything else; he could not see an alternative way to be happy. But then he made the conscious choice to be happy—to make a change and make the best of the cards he had been dealt.

Keith had put his best out there but ultimately had no control over whether he was picked for the draft or not. You cannot choose the circumstances of your life, but you can choose how to react to it or think about it, and that is where the choice to be happy or not comes in. When Keith changed his attitude, he changed his life.

Empowerment is a personal, constant obligation
unique to each of us.

Personal Empowerment is the one thing in life
that cannot be avoided.

No empowerment, no qualifications, no growth.
No growth is a slow road to stagnation.
Don't be a victim of circumstance.
Don't be afraid to take a chance in life.

Fear is a very powerful form of stagnation.

You must keep the engine in drive
and strive for the big prize: *SUCCESS*

Quitting simply is not an option
if you have a real dream and a vision.

Reflections for Remediation, Retention, and Recall . . .

Day 7 - Become Extraordinary

*"Do not wait to strike till the iron is hot;
but make it hot by striking."* William B. Sprague

Yesterday we talked about being willing to change and leaving your comfort zone. Part of being stuck in the status quo is the mistaken belief that to succeed in society we have to be just like everybody else. Let's take a moment to think about the heroes in your life—the people you admire. Would they be considered ordinary or extraordinary? Were Galileo, Gandhi, Mother Teresa, Einstein, Martin Luther King, Jr., or even Elvis or Ray Charles normal, or did they have the courage to break with convention?

There are many things that can stand in the way of happiness and success. Having a negative self-image is certainly one of them. However, a misplaced belief in what you think you need to do to be part of the crowd can be another roadblock that is often overlooked. Renowned motivational writer and speaker Wayne Dyer wrote in his book *Excuses Begone* that we need to make a list of all the things we are "unwilling to do to achieve the life we want"—with the ultimate goal of having a blank sheet.

Jesse Jackson, Shirley Chisholm, Helen Keller, Maya Angelou, Lance Armstrong, Colin Powell, Oprah Winfrey, Magic Johnson, Allen Iverson, Doug Williams, Harriet Tubman, Donnie McClurkin, Robert Schuller, Jackie Robinson, Muhammad Ali, Nelson Mandela—all have faced what appeared to be insurmountable obstacles in their lives, but each had something far stronger than the obstacles, a willingness to win and a desire to *become extraordinary.* Empowered individuals just intend to win. Peace of mind, optimum health, happy relationships, and prosperous ventures are all by-products of the empowerment process to success in life. Start to make the pertinent accommodations and lifestyle assimilations to reach equilibrium. Discover your passion, your true purpose in life, through the personal empowerment process—and don't be afraid to look a little different, unconventional, or even silly in the process!

In each of us there is an opportunity to step beyond our comfort zone just a little bit; and, when you do so, you might surprise yourself and others with just how extraordinary being "abnormal" can be!

**The good times are fine,
they keep a smile on your face.
But the question is this:**

Can You Stand the Rain?

**There is a lot of truth to the statement
*"No Pain, No Gain."***

**Everyone loves
the comfort zone.**

**No one wants to deal with the stress
when something goes wrong.**

**There is a price to pay to keep it sunny each day
Are you willing to pay it?**

Day 8 - Push Beyond Pain

"Pain is just weakness leaving the body" US Marine Corps

You have heard it before "No Pain - No Gain." It is true: nothing worth achieving can be done without work, effort, and some level of sacrifice. Just as a weightlifter cannot build muscle without first tearing down what needs to be built back up. We cannot get to a new you without making some painful mental, physical and emotional changes.

Pain serves a very real purpose. At its most basic level, pain is the ultimate motivator—touch a hot stove, burn your finger, and you won't want to repeat that mistake again. Think about this. When you rest on your foot in the wrong position for too long, it falls asleep. As you start to stretch it out and the blood starts to flow again, it hurts! The longer your foot has been asleep, the more painful it is to wake it up again. The same thing is true on your 30-day path to awakening your Inner Winner. The longer you have been stagnating in the "wrong position," the longer you have been asleep spiritually and emotionally, the more painful your personal awakening can be.

It is simple to stay motivated when things are easy, when our days on our path to growing, mentally, emotionally, and spiritually are sunny. But what about when the days are dark and cloudy? When the rain falls so hard that the path before us seems obliterated and has turned into nothing but an impenetrable slog though the mud, can you stand the rain and push beyond the pain?

Can you stand the rain? What a great metaphor! The famous R&B group New Edition had a hit record in the 90s with that very title. The chorus simply said the same thing I'm saying now, "Sunny days— everybody loves them. But *Can You Stand The Rain*?" When you've planted your seeds for success and set some realistic goals for your mind, body, and spirit, the most difficult thing to do is to remain focused and fired up to achieve them. Every obstacle you could imagine is just waiting to bring the rain down. Well, just remember this, every time the rain falls on Mother Earth, the grass grows greener. Do not let the blurred vision of looking through a rainfall cause you to only see your life's problems, when all that is happening is a momentary challenge that will bring with it new growth when the storm passes!

"No Pain, No Gain." Betty Wright, a successful singer from Miami, famous for her inspirational songs, had a hit about love with that same title. Sometimes you just have got to go through some pain to gain love's reward for patience and perseverance. When I entered graduate school in 1991, I had more rain and pain coming down than you could ever imagine. I was working full time as a musician six nights a week, working as a substitute teacher three to five days a week, raising Jonathan, who was only a year old, and attending classes from eight to five every Saturday. There were times when I just wanted to quit!

The rain and the pain were creating a stress that was almost an insurmountable test. But I saw the light at the end. I kept the focus! I knew this, too, would eventually come to an end. Even after I graduated and had to take twenty more hours of classes and pass some grueling state exams to get my teacher certification, I never lost sight of the light at the end of the tunnel. For that, I will always be grateful to Dr. Arlene Sacks, one of my graduate school professors, for believing in me when I just wanted to quit. All she said was "You've come too far to turn back now!" She also reminded me occasionally, "This too will pass." She and all the beautiful ladies from Barry University Graduate School were my angels who inspired me to look for the sunshine, to grow from the rain, and to push past my pain.

**You're a winner if you got up today and
you have somehow made it through the day.**

**You're winning if you found the journey along the way
is more important than the destination.**

**You know a winner when he or she speaks
only with positive energy to everyone.**

A winner knows there's always today to begin again.

**A winner lets yesterday be water
that has passed under the bridge of life.**

**A winner knows it is never too late to
make the revision to have the vision of a winner!!**

Day 9 - Seize the Day

"Carpe Diem. Seize the day, boys. Make your lives extraordinary"- Professor John Keating, Robin Williams' character in <u>Dead Poet's Society</u>

With every day, with each new sunrise, we are given a renewed opportunity to make a positive change, to make a difference in our lives or in the lives of others. Each dawn brings with it another opportunity to remain ordinary or to become extraordinary. Seize the day!

Despite what you may think, winning is not something only other people can do. We can all be winners, and it takes only one thing—effort. What makes a winner? In athletics, physical strength helps, of course, and drive, stamina, perseverance—all of those things. But winners on and off the playing field have something else in common—creativity!

Creativity is defined as *the ability to transcend traditional ideas, rules, patterns, relationships, or the like, and to create meaningful new ideas, forms, methods, interpretations, etc.*

I believe that what gives winners the power to seize the day is not some superhuman qualities that help them achieve their goals, but rather their ability to go beyond the traditional way of thinking. We all may define winning in our own unique ways, but we all want to win!

How many times do you hear news reporters hail the runner-up from the Super Bowl, the NBA championship, or the World Series? They don't give the runner up to the New York marathon any of the grand prizes the winner gets, even though there may be less than a minute between the first and second place times. The winner takes all. Ask Derek Jeter of the New York Yankees. All he's ever wanted to do is win. He was drafted out of high school and paid $800,000 a year, and now he makes $20 million a year, has earned five World Series rings, and endorses a host of products. Winners simply love to win! Isn't it your time?

When my son Jonathan was 10 years old, I coached his optimist basketball team. Most of the kids were beginners. Their parents just wanted their kids to play basketball; they didn't really care about winning. The kids had a different attitude. Even though they weren't that great, they knew we kept a score and that there was a championship. They also were aware of the fact that everybody loves a winner! They wanted to win! Winning builds self-esteem, no matter your age. I would always ask the kids a simple question right before the game. We'd get in the huddle, and I'd ask them: "How bad do you want it?" Invariably, they would say: "Real bad, Coach!!"

How bad do you want it?

STRIVE!

STUDY, STUDY, STUDY!

TRY MY VERY BEST TO PASS LIFE'S TESTS!

RETAIN AND RECALL ALL THAT I CAN!

INNOVATE AND INVENT WITH POSITIVE INTENT!

VISUALIZE SUCCESS!

EMPOWER AND EDUCATE MYSELF FOREVER!

Day 10 – STRIVE for Victory

"Accept challenges, so that you may feel the exhilaration of victory." George S. Patton

The process of building self-esteem through self-affirmation begins with dismissing our negative scripts. What are negative scripts? These are the internal dialogues that keep us down, that are filled with "I cant's," and are peppered with negative statements and beliefs about ourselves that prevent victory.

True self-esteem also comes with an understanding that we cannot do everything great, but that everybody is great at something. This is a core tenet of the self-affirmation theory. If you tell me that I can't sing very well, I will just go and play my guitar instead, which I know I am better at. If you say my guitar playing is still off, I'll go shoot some baskets, because I know my basketball game is better than my guitar chords and so on, and so on. Practice these kinds of self-affirming behaviors every day, and you are bound for victory!

Make the acronym **STRIVE** a daily affirmation process. Simply put these two words in front of the sentence on the preceding page for each letter of the acronym:
I WILL __ __ __ __ __ __!

If you make this a daily routine, you'll always keep your internal dialogue positive and the universe will accommodate your requests. If you **S**tudy, **T**ry, **R**etain, **I**nnovate, **V**isualize and **E**mpower your mind, body and spirit every day, you will reach **GOALS** that will propel you to the next level in your life.

Imagine walking into your office or classroom and feeling like you own the room! You're on top of the world! You're exhibiting your **OPA** factor (Optimum Physical Appearance). It is easier to feel good about yourself when you like what you see in the mirror. It is not vain to want to look your best to feel your best. Your body is your temple; respect it! Remember that your path to victory involves remaking yourself in mind, body and spirit. The three go hand-in-hand.

STRIVE for greatness every day in every way. I do! I love it.
I'm training for my sixteenth marathon. I think I might try a triathlon
next! I'm 56! Come on. Just STRIVE for it. It's a lot closer than you
think!!

You're here to make your contribution.

**Know that your existence in this time and
place isn't just a coincidence.**

**For this reason, enjoy the moment,
maximize the opportunity and
never regret anything or anyone.**

**Life is just too short to have a perception
that is blurred by
negative thoughts or negative people.**

**Know that there's only good in your life.
Absolute good.**

**It's time to find your passion,
your purpose in life.**

**Make the contribution to the universe
that only you could make.**

Day 11 – Make a Difference

"Every charitable act is a stepping-stone toward heaven."
Henry Ward Beecher

"Do Unto Others," the words of the Golden Rule, are not only great words to live by, but helping others can also be one of the keys to achieving your own success and happiness. We are all put here for a reason—to make a contribution. The best way to make your contribution is to find your passion. What is the one thing you would do in life if you knew you couldn't fail? If you can answer this question without a shadow of doubt, then you've discovered your passion and purpose for your contribution to life. If you cannot answer this question, then now is the time to explore the possibilities.

One of the best ways that I can think of to help you find that passion, and your purpose in life, is through volunteerism. There are those of us who are innately selfless, who have a fundamental need to help those less fortunate than themselves. Those individuals have my thanks and the thanks of the millions they have helped. But for the rest of us, I put it to you that helping others is also a great way to help yourself.

Simply stated, it feels good to help other people. And while the very nature of volunteering is giving of oneself without expecting anything in return, those who give back receive quite a bit as well. Helping others can help you to find your place in the world. Volunteering builds self-esteem and can make you feel that you are doing your part to make the world a better place, and the truth is that you probably are.

Don't stagnate! Activate your opportunities in life with optimum awareness and a positive attitude to give to the universe and you will naturally begin finding what you seek in life. I love to perform and speak. I love to teach and coach. I've found that my contributions are always going to be associated with giving back to people and humanity in the form of information and multi-entertainment services. That's why I've written this book of empowering inspirations, motivations, and strategic alternatives for enhanced productivity.

Call it the Golden Rule, Karma, or the simple realization of "what goes around comes around." *It's your time to assess and find what you were meant to give to the universe; in so giving, you, too, will receive.*

You must affirm your oneness:

I am one with love, peace and understanding from my constant innate source.

Wherever I am, the Source is.

My past has no power over me.

My true reality lies in the *here and now*.

Nothing or no one can keep me from realizing this truth.

The Source and I are one. I can never be separated from it!

Day 12 – Connect to the Power of Belief

"I can't believe that God put us on this earth to be ordinary." Lou Holtz

We have now spent more than 10 days on a path designed to change the way we think about success, the ways we think about the world around us, and, most importantly, how we think about ourselves. I have shared with you stories and words of inspiration that, if you have read this far, you have surely come to realize that they are intended to do one thing—help you develop a positive mindset. Developing the ability to think more positively is the most powerful life strategy there is.

A key to thinking positively is believing not only in yourself, but in confirming on a daily basis that you have the ability to accomplish whatever it is that you want. New Age pundits, life coaches, and motivational speakers such as myself like to call this removal of self-doubt "affirmation." Using the powerful techniques of self-affirmation, CEOs and successful entrepreneurs have gained power over their competition and Olympic athletes have broken world records. On a personal level, positive affirmation will transform your life, improve your health, and renew your joy and passion for living. Self-affirmation allows you to wake up each morning overflowing with excitement, energy, and joy, and to be better able to face each day!

All that is true, but long before we modern motivators coined the idea of "affirmation," there was, and still is, another power that does the same thing—prayer. I am not going to get all preachy on you now and say that you need to pray to this God or another, but I will say this, you cannot succeed in life or accomplish any of the goals I will lay out for you over the remaining days of our journey without some kind of faith.

Faith is that common thread among all religions—a belief in something greater than ourselves. Self-affirmation is a wonderful thing, but its true strength lies in the belief that the greatest strength comes from something beyond us. It is through prayer, faith, or affirmations that we stay connected to that source and ultimately tie into its power. It's been said there are no atheists in foxholes. I have known many people—otherwise totally non-religious—who, when faced with tight situations, have told me they got through them by praying. It wasn't even that they necessarily prayed to God; they just prayed. And in that moment, they knew they had drawn on greater power, and it was that faith that allowed them to move forward.

Interestingly enough, recently even highly regarded institutions like Duke and Harvard University not only have begun accepting the healing power of prayer and positive thinking, but are actually finding ways to study and document it. In Florida, at the University of Miami, AIDS researcher Gail Ironson may be one of the first scientists who has actually documented a connection between spirituality and the progression of disease. Ironson studied patients since the 1990s who were HIV positive but never developed AIDS, and she found that the commonality was a strong belief in the Divine. While these studies seem to indicate there is at least some anecdotal evidence of the power of faith, I am reminded of "Pascal's Wager" proposed by famous French philosopher Blasé Pascal, which, simply put, states that since science and reason can never adequately prove the existence of God, we should all live our lives as if there is a God, because we have everything to gain by doing so and absolutely nothing to lose.

As a teacher, I am familiar with the three R's. Instead, let me present you with the four I's. The source of faith is *innate, intrinsic, inherent,* and *inborn.* Faith can't work if you do not internalize it. The Source is as close as the air that you breathe if you'll just believe! My mother took me to church from the age of five until I left home for college at seventeen. My foundation for dealing with anything in life is grounded on the principle of faith from the source. I don't know how many times in my life I've been faced with circumstances that just seemed to be out of my control. The only hope I had of seeing a favorable outcome was to just turn within and accept that my internal dialogue with my source would guide me in the right direction.

To this day, as an adult, my faith has taken me through the storms of my life. As a marathon runner I have to reach deep inside when the wall comes up after the twentieth mile. It becomes mind over matter. The Source has to be there for me. At the age of 50, I ran the New York City marathon. It was my ninth marathon. My training regime was somewhat stagnated by injury with less than two months to race day. I started to swim and run less, to give my leg time to heal. When I did start to run again, I experienced the same problem with my leg muscles collapsing.

This time, I decided to reach within and find the strength from my Source to keep my focus and complete the run. My strategy changed to one that required me to slow down, even if I had to walk the final minutes and just have faith that I could finish—and I did! The very same thing happened to me thirty minutes into the NYC marathon. I didn't get my best time, but I did complete the marathon in 4:40. My personal marathon record is 3:29.

The Source!
You can't leave home without it!!

When the *UNIQUE* you opens the door
for the creative you to come shining through,
something great happens!!
The *GENIUS* comes out to play for a day!

Your personal contribution represents
the intrinsic, the inherent,
unique genius that's innate in you.

Imagination is an incredible tool to use
24 hours a day, 7 days a week, 365 days a year!

The genius is working even when you're sleeping.
Remember, time is like money.

Don't waste it! Spend it wisely
discover the *GENIUS*!

Reflections for Remediation, Retention, and Recall . .

Day 13 – Find Your Inner Genius

"I have nothing to declare but my genius." Oscar Wilde

When you think of a genius, what immediately comes to mind? I think to most people it is the iconic wild-haired image of Albert Einstein. Certainly intelligence is one measure of genius. But haven't Mozart, Beethoven, or Stevie Wonder and Quincy Jones for that matter, been referred to as musical geniuses? While MIT unquestionably puts out its fair share of geniuses, I would prefer to define genius the way well known motivational speaker Robert Kiyosaki, author of the *Rich Dad/Poor Dad* program, does. That genius is not so much about how smart you are, but is about finding what it is you are the most passionate about in life. When you do that, when you find what it is that you love, you cannot help but become a genius at it!

So what does this have to do with being successful? Two very important things. First, if we recognize our genius and our talent, we can focus our career goals on doing that thing that we love. Even if that thing is something as simple as baking cookies. Do the names Famous Amos or Mrs. Fields mean anything to you? Second, even if you find your talent and your passion and it turns out to be something that you do not think that you can translate into a career under any circumstances, your life is still richer when you embrace it. In this way, you will get to feel, see, and taste what playing with your inner genius feels like—and recognize it when it comes knocking!

How many times have you had an idea that appeared to be a great opportunity to become an entrepreneur and you quickly shot it down? It's in those very moments of creative bliss that we accept or reject the genius at the door of life. How many times are you going to say, "If I could have done X, maybe I would have been Y?" Every time you procrastinate the possibility of succeeding or failing, you've only fed another negative thought to stagnate your glory. Have you let the innate power to be all that you've dreamed of just die?

It's time for a creative resurrection. Come on! Let the genius come out to play! I know that typically we only associate genius with high intelligence, but please don't confuse genius with a high IQ. I read a short story about the greatness that singer/songwriter Lionel Richie manifested in less than an hour for one of his most successful songs. "Easy" was written on a tour bus in just thirty minutes. You see, you don't know when the genius wants to come out and play. Just be a good sport and get in the game of life; don't be afraid to take a chance, be silly, or be ridiculed. If your inner genius is trying to tell you something, listen! Because your inner genius speaks to what you are passionate about – and what you are passionate about is who you are and who you can be.

There are countless billionaires who got where they are today by being focused, hard-working individuals with the ability to recognize when the unique genius is ready to play. Just ask Sam Walton, the great talent behind Wal-Mart. The genius inside asked him to come and play discount store owner. The rest is history. Boy, did he come to play!

We are what we think about ourselves. Every physical action has been thought about internally long before it becomes an external exhibition.

It's very important to keep thoughts positive. Remember it's still a choice to get back what you give to the universe.

Positive thoughts generate positive feedback and good vibrations from most situations. How are you vibrating? How have your thoughts been lately?

Negatives are only obscure distractions from the main attraction— the positive, the absolute good in life.

Day 14 – Think Positively

"Think positive for thoughts lead to words; speak positively, for words become actions. Act positively for actions lead to your Destiny!" Arun Gandhi

"The Power of Positive Thinking" How many times have you heard that? So much so that it almost has became a motivational speaker's cliché. However, let me tell you something about clichés, we may sometimes groan at them, but another word for a cliché is a truism. And there is no one thing, no point, I can make clearer to you then this; if you want to change your life, you must dispense with negativity.

Just as you can train your arms to be stronger, you can train your mind to think more positively. Some people use prayer, and if that is what works for you, more power to you. But you can use any kind of repetition of positive words or affirmations to bring your mind, body, and sprit to a more positive place. Close your eyes, relax, breathe deeply and rhythmically and concentrate solely on the positive things in your life. Your kids, your health, whatever it may be—just let go of the negative and focus on the good things in your life. You know they are there! Do this every day, ritually, when you wake up. This will train your subconscious, the very fiber of your being, to be more positive. It is like building up muscle to face physical challenges, or pumping up your immune system to fight disease. Constant positive affirmation builds up your inner strength to fight negativity!

Ancient philosophers, motivational speakers, and psychologists alike say that one of the greatest limiting factors we put on ourselves is negativity. Negativity breeds fear; negativity saps your strength and the strength of those around you. Unfortunately, we are often bombarded by negativity. Throughout our lives, certainly we hear the words "no" or "you can't do that" far more often than we hear encouragement. Yet, those who are truly successful in their lives or careers purge themselves of negativity.

As a teacher, coach/athlete, entertainer, speaker, entrepreneur and a parent raising a teenager, I'm constantly faced with random situations that demand quick, firm decisions. If my internal dialogue is full of negative energy and gives voice to possible pessimistic outcomes, then there is no possible outcome other than a life plunged into a field of constant chaos. How many times have you had a bad feeling about a situation only to have it manifest itself in your life just the way you'd thought about it happening. I'm sure that you could have dismissed the negative thoughts and focused on the positive possibilities instead. I started to run marathons at age 43, when I also became a girls cross-country coach at Flanagan High in 1996.

Long before I decided to approach the cross-country coach to ask if he needed an assistant with the over thirty boys and girls on the team, I had negative internal dialogues to talk myself out of the possibility of coaching or running a marathon. I was over forty years old and had a four-year-old son to raise. It wasn't until my thoughts were focused on the positive possibilities and benefits of running every day with the girls and concurrently training for the Walt Disney Marathon that I was able to step out on faith and keep my thoughts full of good about my decision. Here I am, ten years later, still running marathons after coaching for seven years, and seeing my son Jonathan come to Flanagan and run cross country. Just my thoughts alone could have changed it all!!

Nothing could be more gratifying than the thrill of enthusiasm. It's just a time to feel free.

Enthusiasm ignites feelings of sheer delight to this place of spiritual heights!

WOW! Oh how we wish life was always sunny days, bright smiles and laughter in the hearts of all.

For every young mind that hadn't been blemished by life's hard falls, there is an unconditional answer to enthusiasm's call.

There is no fear factor to obscure the thoughts, just thoughts of having a good time, a good life!

Winner takes all---be it big or small.

How many enthusiastic moments have you had lately?

Day 15 – Embrace Your Enthusiasm

"Enthusiasm is contagious. Be a carrier."
Susan G. Rabin

Yesterday we talked about releasing negativity. You might intuitively say that the flip-side of the coin of negativity is being positive or optimistic, but the true antithesis of negativity is enthusiasm. Enthusiasm is more than just being positive as opposed to negative. Enthusiasm is positive thinking on steroids. Enthusiasm is embracing life and all of its richness. Enthusiasm is knowing when to let go, kick off your shoes, and run through the Park Fountains—or dance as if nobody is looking.

Faith and enthusiasm are very interconnected. True faith means having a powerful belief in who and what you are. The word enthusiasm actually comes from the Greek word "enthousiasmos," which literally translates into *being inspired or possessed by a divine being*. That should give you some idea about just what a powerful force the ancient philosophers believed enthusiasm to be. The expression "faith moves mountains" can just as easily be applied to being enthusiastic. Enthusiasm is a driving force to create momentum. Enthusiasm is empowering spiritually, mentally and physically; it creates an overall feeling of happiness and well-being that can actually be infectious!

Dale Carnegie, the father of all motivational speakers, said, "Act enthusiastic and you will be enthusiastic." It may not exactly be that simple, but enthusiasm does work like a self-generating perpetual motion engine. Acting enthusiastically outwardly—smiling, being upbeat and energetic—will actually trigger these same emotions internally, becoming a cycle. Once you start to feel more enthusiastic, you will then continue to act more enthusiastically and so on and so on.

Enthusiasm not only will improve your general outlook on life, but it also has some very practical effects as well. Enthusiasm destroys fear and nervousness, it is the most powerful antidote to procrastination I have yet to find. It is also the ultimate stress buster. Sometimes we have to take a chill pill on life. Taking anything too seriously too long will lead us down a road to the stress zone. We should stay focused on our goals, but we also have to know when to lighten up a little.

We're all guilty of an all-work-and-no-play attitude sometimes. In September 2000, I went to the hospital with extreme chest pains early one morning when I could barely walk back to my classroom after a fire drill. I spent four days in the hospital being monitored, and was given stress tests and every other test associated with heart failure to ensure I was okay. I personally took the experience as a wake up call to eliminate the stress and initiate more moments of enthusiasm and relaxation. My doctor said my physical health was just fine, but the stress I'd experienced would only get worse if I did not eliminate the source. Maybe there are some signs of stress in your life that indicate you need to take a personal analysis. When was the last time you just took it easy?

Are there stressors taking you further away from a stress-free, enthusiastic day? Are there people in your personal or business life who consistently create a stressful environment for you?

Remember, you are the Captain of the ship. No one can board without your permission. Why not make more choices that reflect enthusiasm rather than stress? The more moments of enthusiasm we experience, the more we experience the spirit in each of us. The opposite prevails in stress-related encounters. We just get further away from the sunshine if every day we feel stress.

Why do we have to make the road we travel so much more difficult than it has to be?

Who are the people you call your friends?

Are you trying to get in where you don't fit in?

Relationships are like a pair of shoes.
If you force your feet into a pair of shoes that don't fit, you'll surely feel the pain later.

Relationships are no different!

54

Day 16 – Build a Circle of Support

"I'll get by with a little help from my friends"
Lennon/McCartney

You have come this far, now take a deep breath and feel proud that you've reached the halfway mark to the new you. You probably already see some improvement—and I bet the people around you do too. In this chapter we will talk a little bit more about the people around you—the relationships in your life. No one succeeds in a vacuum. Not only can we not do it alone, but to achieve our goals, we need to surround ourselves with the right people.

I opened this chapter with the lines from a well-known popular song. Here is another: *Lean on me, when you're not strong, and I'll be your friend, I'll help you carry on. For it won't be long, 'til I'm gonna need – somebody to lean on...* These familiar words of Bill Withers' inspirational classic ring very true when it comes to achieving goals and solving problems. I have found that one of the most successful ways to achieve your personal goals is to share them with others.

Let's face it - everyone I know loves to give advice. And when you share a problem, or a goal with another—whether you actually ask for it or not—one of the first things they will do is offer you some advice. What they tell you may not always be good advice, but sharing goals with others opens up a wealth of possibilities and options you may not have considered and encourages others to share their experiences with reaching the same goal. Sharing goals also brings a fresh outlook or perspective to your problem or goal. The person you share the goal with may have access to resources you do not have, new ideas, or untapped abilities related to the situation.

But there is always the question of when and with whom to share your dreams and your life. That is a very big question and one I could devote an entire book to! For now, let me say this: you may not ever get back that which is given from the heart in every relationship, but that should never stop you from giving or sharing. I know it's easier said than done, but remember that we're all very fragile when it comes to matters of the heart. Remember our discussion of the Source? The Source lives in the heart.

Like many, I discovered early in life how fragile the heart can be. I decided to let someone in too far, too soon! When she decided it was time to move on and let me go, I thought I'd never love anyone that way ever again. I was only sixteen and Veronica was the junior class queen. I felt like a king for a while, but she ultimately dismissed me for another guy. At the time, I felt that I was never again going to let someone have that kind of emotional power over me.

It took some time, but of course, I got over Veronica. But what the experience taught me early on was just how deeply a relationship that on the surface appears only physical can affect the mind, body and sprit, both positively and negatively. That early experience taught me that, yes, the human heart is fragile and relationships can hurt, but we also need them. No one is an island.

I'm still learning from my experiences! You never know it all. You just try to arm the body, mind, and spirit by learning from experience. Yes, we fall down, but we can always get up and get back in the game— even the relationship game. And if we get hurt? Then we can get by with a little help from our friends.

**When you know only your absolute best will
pass the test, this is when greatness will manifest!**

**The road to greatness may be long and lonely,
but the rewards are only for a chosen few!**

Who knows? The next great one could be YOU.

Forget about the destination…Just endure the journey.

**When you finally arrive,
you will find the place for the next great one!**

Day 17 – Say "I AM the Greatest"

"I am the greatest; I said that even before I knew I was."
Muhammad Ali

How can we start any chapter about greatness with a quote from anyone other than Muhammad Ali? Sports enthusiasts will agree for generations to come that he was great, and may argue about what it was that made him so. We can go on and on about his knockouts, his footwork, his blinding speed, and, of course, his showmanship. But Ali's true greatness begins and ends with his own unshakable belief in it.

I believe that everyone has that kind of greatness in them. It is a seed, filled with unlimited potential that is nurtured through passion, and as we have said in previous chapters, often it takes pain and sacrifice to bring your greatness to fruition. Believe in your Greatness. And do not confuse that belief with being conceited or egotistical. Do not be afraid to shine! There is nothing arrogant about being the best at what you do!

Marianne Williamson wrote in her book *A Return to Love: Reflections on the Principles of A Course in Miracles:*

Our deepest fear is not that we are inadequate. Our deepest fear is that we are powerful beyond measure. It is our Light, not our darkness, that most frightens us. We ask ourselves, who am I to be brilliant, gorgeous, talented, fabulous? Actually, who are you not to be? You are a child of God. You playing small does not serve the world. There is nothing enlightening about shrinking so that other people won't feel insecure around you. We were born to make manifest the glory of God that is within us. It is not just in some of us, it is in everyone. And, as we let our own Light shine, we unconsciously give other people permission to do the same. As we are liberated from our own fear, our presence automatically liberates others.

Do you know how many times Walt Disney went bankrupt before the Magic Kingdom became the most successful tourist attraction in the world?

Did you know that Michael Jordan didn't make his high school basketball team the first time he tried out?

Do you know how many times he took the last shot to win a game and missed?

Do you really think the Wright brothers took flight on the first try?

The universe is just waiting on the next great one. Come on! Get busy! Maybe, just maybe, you're next! Who knows what the future holds? All you can do it reach for it with a positive "I can win and find my greatness in the process" attitude.

Donald Trump didn't become one of the world's most successful real estate entrepreneurs overnight. He had to buy and make one deal at a time. You think Donald didn't have some obstacles to overcome? Donald realized early in the real estate game that greatness comes with a price. Are you willing to pay the price for YOUR GREATNESS?

I'm a professional entertainer. I make a decent living singing and playing bass guitar in the top clubs in South Florida. This is my 22nd year in the industry. I started playing in nightclubs when I was only 16. My brother, Nelson, and sister, Pansy, were my managers. We had a lead singer who was only 12 years old. She was my baby sister, Ruby—the great one! Ruby discovered her greatness at a very early age and began to enjoy the journey and keep her eye on the destination—SUCCESS! Of all the jobs and opportunities she had, nothing has ever taken her away from the greatness that is her voice. You see, Ruby is a classic, one of the chosen ones who has the innate gift for song. Her car reads: BORN TO SING! Ruby always feels she missed something by not going to college. I just remind her that the great ones have something far more important than all the degrees in the world—a gift from GOD to give to the world! I thank my Mom for God's great gift to this world—her baby girl, Ruby! Here's to you, Ruby, because we love you! You are the next Great One!

It is not what you have that counts,
it is what you do with what you've got!

The only limitations that exist
are the ones you place upon yourself.

If you say "I can't"
there is not a chance for you to win.

But if you say "I can," then it's a sure shot
that you'll give it all you've got to WIN!!!

Think about it!
You are what you think of yourself
regardless of what anyone else thinks or says.

Reflections for Remediation, Retention, and Recall . . .

Day 18 – Stop Arguing For Your Limitations

*"Argue for your limitations – and sure enough
they are yours." Richard Bach*

How many times did you want to try something new, take advantage of a possibly amazing, albeit risky, opportunity and heard that old familiar voice inside that says, "No, I can't." You convince yourself that you are too old, not smart enough, and not strong enough, etc. While you argue for those limitations, the opportunity passes and we remain in the safe status quo.

Of course, not all limits are necessarily a bad thing. Speed limits save lives, and there is surely wisdom in respecting certain physical limitations. If you are allergic to bee stings, there is nothing to be gained by sticking your arm in a beehive. On the other hand, there are those among us who are even able to break the bonds of what would appear to be physical limitations. In 2001, Erik Weihenmayer became the only blind person in history to climb Mount Everest. We have all seen the martial artist who can break a concrete block with his head and the yogi master who can walk unscathed across a floor of burning embers. What do they all have in common? A belief in themselves that goes beyond limits.

It is the limitations that we put on ourselves that keep our genius and our greatness trapped in the box! Come on! Let them out to play! Your comfort zone is the reason you can't fly! There is truly no limitation to reaching your maximum potential. Remember the Little Engine That Could? Try saying "I can" enough to get tough. Yes, I know the road is going to be rough, but that's not an excuse to just give up. What appears to be going wrong is just a moment of growth.

As the world famous rapper and entrepreneur Master P would say: "There's no limit!" Master P had a vision when he was faced with an environment that gave him no reason for living. Against all the odds, he was determined to be a successful athlete and businessman. Not only did he form his own record label "No Limit" and become one of the most successful rappers of the decade, he also realized his dream to play professional basketball. He refused to accept limitations. He simply said,

"I can! I will!" Master P's son is also a rapper, and Master P is his producer. Both are now doing movies and Master P is a very wealthy and successful entrepreneur simply because he refused to accept labels and limitations.

Have you placed limitations upon yourself because of your environment, race, socio- economic situation or disability? I know that it's difficult to have a vision in the darkness. The odds just don't seem to be favorable, but Reverend Joel Osteen speaks about God's favor in his incredible book, *Your Best Life Now!* If you claim it in the spirit, it will manifest itself in your physical world. Just start by simply saying, "I can! I will! I have to win and there are no limitations!!"

Dream big. Understand that there is absolutely nothing you cannot do once you put your mind, heart, and soul into it. *Stop arguing for your limitations,* let go of your fears, and go ahead and fail. If you can do that, you can overcome the only thing that can get in the way of achieving your goals—*yourself.*

**If you do not believe in yourself
why would you expect anyone else to believe in you?**

You are one of a kind.

Everyone has a light under the sun.

Let yours shine brightly!

Day 19 – Believe in Yourself

"To be what we are, and to become what we are capable of becoming, is the only purpose of life."
Robert Lewis Stevenson

Think about this. Have you ever taken a long trip in your car somewhere and suddenly awakened from a fog, finding yourself at your destination with almost no recollection of how you got there or without remembering a single piece of scenery you passed along the way? Too many of us go through life the same way: stuck in a mental, physical, and spiritual fog—on autopilot. So let me ask you this: do you want to get to the end of your life's journey and realize you can't remember what you passed along the way? Maybe breaking out of that fog is what brought you to this book in the first place.

This is where the decision to live *consciously* begins. It is where you start to make the conscious choice between just being alive and living! Today we turn off the cruise control, break out of the negative patterns of thought and behavior that blind us to who we are and to who we can be. We start living consciously by believing in ourselves!

By believing in yourself you gain the ability to choose the life you want to live. When you remove self-doubt in this way you gain back power and control over your own life. With self-belief, you become in charge. You are in command and steer your own path to your destiny— instead of being driven figuratively and literally by the autopilot of your subconscious doubts. To see the light, you must first believe in yourself, and never stop believing. To keep the car analogy going, believing in yourself is like the key that turns the ignition; positive thoughts keep the battery strong and the engine running!

Cars now have computers to send reminders when imbalance occurs with a warning light to get service or risk a breakdown. We get signals in life from the Source. Don't ignore your life's check engine light! It's an intuitive reminder that something isn't right. Listen to your intuition! Believe in yourself.

Unfavorable circumstances have a way of pulling us into the dark tunnel of despair. The further we fall, the darker and deeper the tunnel gets. You lose a job, a relationship goes bad, your health starts to fail, or you have just lost a battle with one of life's multiple challenges. You can run if you'd like, but you cannot hide from life's challenging rides. They're all part of the journey. However, believing in yourself when they occur will only make you stronger.

When I was sleeping on the floor and taking a bath in the back yard under a hose hanging from a tree in Liberty City, in the heart of a rough area of Miami in 1981, I had a very low fuel tank of faith. All I could see and feel was life not being fair to me. I had no money, no job, and was having a hard time trying to keep the light on to make it through it all. But, you see, I never stopped believing that this too would pass and that my mission to be a successful musician would let my light shine. I wasn't alone. There were seven of us trying to make it, and many of the days were very, very long. But one day, someone I'd met along the way sent me a gift that showed up in an unexpected way: a leather jacket, some money, and a small bible with a letter that I still have to this day as a reminder that the source is guiding me everyday.

I eventually recorded an album and moved on in my life; I am proud to say I survived the challenge and saw the light. I never stopped believing. When you just BELIEVE against all the odds, the Source's light will shine through it all. NEVER STOP BELIEVING IN YOURSELF!

Be truly optimistic! It's the ultimate step
To a foundation for success in life!

Optimism defeats any opportunity
For thoughts of lack and limitation
to create negative, pessimistic,
stagnating energy.

Optimistic people always have a vision
of light shining at the end of the tunnel
as a reminder that nothing can stop them
from reaching the next level.

Energize your thoughts with powerful optimism.
Be patient. Stay in active pursuit.

Be optimistic for a successful outcome!

It's always closer than you think!

Reflections for Remediation, Retention, and Recall . . .

Day 20 – Keep On The Sunnyside

"Life is a grindstone. Whether it grinds us down or polishes us up depends on us." Thomas L. Holdcroft

Optimism is more than just thinking positively and being enthusiastic. We have covered both of those concepts already. Thinking positively and acting enthusiastically are reflections of optimism, or ways to remain optimistic in the face of adversity, but optimism itself is a fundamental way of life for successful people.

A recent study found that more than 50% of Americans are pessimistic—their outlook on life is that things are bad and will just continue to get worse. The same study, which was published in WebMD, said that optimists not only will far and away be happier and more successful then their pessimistic counterparts, but they actually lead healthier lives. The study said those with a positive outlook lived longer and were less prone to heart disease, cancer, and other serious ailments. Psychologists have also found that our brains are not hard-wired to be positive or negative. Optimism and pessimism are learned behaviors, and you can learn to be more optimistic. Martin Seligman, author of the book *Authentic Happiness* says we can "learn to control whether that glass is half empty or half full." When you hear the stories of successful people, they may be very different in origin and diverse in each endeavor, but there's one thing that's universal: They're always *optimistic,* no matter the circumstances. They stay in the game. An optimist will never lose sight of the light at the end of the tunnel.

Professional actors and singers such as Jim Carey, Jennifer Lopez, Britney Spears, R. Kelly, Keenan Ivory Wayans, Halle Berry, Chris Rock, Eddie Murphy, Madonna, Whitney Houston, Queen Latifah, Donny McClurkin, Beyonce, and Fantasia certainly faced challenges. I've personally seen them on television or heard them speak on radio about their struggles. They just refused to quit. For each of them, giving up was just not an option.

When I made a very serious decision to pursue a career in the music industry in June 1976, I had just gotten my degree in business administration from Florida A & M University. I'd been playing bass guitar in bands since I was 16 and I loved it. I packed everything I owned and got on the back of a U-Haul truck and went to Newark, New Jersey to pursue a recording deal for my band. Believe it or not, I had a record contract six months later against any odds you could imagine. You see, we refused to quit and the universe just seemed to answer the call.

After being with my band for well over a decade, I decided to leave, get married, and start a new life in Miami. Against all the odds, over twenty years later, I'm still doing what I like to do. I play my bass and sing for a living only because I've always remained optimistic and refuse to quit.

I remember coming home from one of my performances and watching a late night infomercial from Carlton Sheets on how to get into real estate with no money down. One night I decided to buy the money-back program and try my luck. I procrastinated for months before I finally made a firm optimistic commitment to dive in and go the distance. In one year, I not only bought a $300,000 apartment building, I also bought a duplex with less than $3,000. All the investments happened with (OPM): Other People's Money. I will not tell you it was easy, because it wasn't. But I will tell you it wasn't impossible because I was optimistic and persistent in my belief. I'm still in the game.

I refuse to quit! Be optimistic! It works if you work it!

Tips on How to be More Optimistic

- **Learn to Meditate** - Brain mapping studies of people during meditation have actually proven that the centers of the brain that are responsible for positive emotions are stimulated during meditation. Meditation is also a great process through which to give yourself your daily affirmations and concentrate on developing a more positive inner voice.

- **The Power of Threes** – Psychologists have found that it takes three positive thoughts or inactions to counter one negative experience. So next time you are feeling overwhelmed, listen to your favorite tune, have an ice cream or other comfort food, and pet your dog or cat. You will start feeling much better!

- **Documentation** – The best way to be optimistic and stay that way is to keep an "Optimism Journal." At the end of each day, write down at least three good things that happened to you that day and explain why they happened.

Your worst enemy to success is FEAR!!

In order to be a peak performer under pressure, you must learn to feel the fear and believe that you can still get the job accomplished anyway.

To believe is to have FAITH.

DO IT! N.O.W.
(Remember: No Other Way!)

Reflections for Remediation, Retention, and Recall . . .

Day 21 – Overcome Your Fears

"For God hath not given us the spirit of fear; but of power, and of love, and of a sound mind." II Timothy 1:7

"Anything I've ever done that ultimately was worthwhile initially scared me to death!" Betty Bender

Let's revisit fear for a moment. Fear does serve a purpose. And there are times when fear is a good thing. If our ancestors on the plains of Africa did not have a healthy fear of lions, and tigers, and bears, we wouldn't be here right now talking about success in life! But when you look at whatever it is that is keeping you from doing something, somewhere among the reasons for not doing that thing, for not moving forward, for stagnating—is fear.

Back on Day 4 we discussed how it is not failure, but the fear of failure that holds most people back. Today I would like to share with you five time-honored ways of overcoming your fears.

1 - Face Your Fear! Eleanor Roosevelt said, "You gain strength, courage, and confidence by every experience in which you really stop to look fear in the face." This remarkable woman was 100% correct! Every time you face a fear, you gain those three qualities: strength, courage, and confidence. The bigger the fear, the more you have to gain. You will find that when you face your biggest fears and survive them, you will soon have the strength, courage and confidence to face anything!

2 - Get Busy! Inaction breeds fear. Stop sitting in the house with the covers over your head waiting for courage to come to you—get moving. The more you stand still, the more time you have to think about your fears and the more time you give the monsters you create inside of your head to take control!

3 - Get Real! Do a reality check. You know why phobias are called irrational fears? Because that is what they are—irrational! What about the things you are afraid of? Is there a real rational basis for that fear? There could be, but more often than not, there isn't. On closer examination, you may find that fear is based on not seeing the whole picture, on misinterpretation, or on lies!

4 - Let Go! Stop clinging to your illusion of safety. This is the same idea of stepping out of your comfort zone. What is safety after all? Do you think you are really safe where you are in the status quo? Do you think you can't lose your job? Are you sure that your company can't go out of business? Things happen, and they can always happen anytime to anybody. Security is just an illusion. It was Helen Keller who said, "Security is mostly a superstition. It does not exist in nature. Life is either a daring adventure or nothing."

5 - Be Curious! Curiosity will conquer fear as surely as courage. Being fearful means you are all closed up. You put up walls between yourself and the world to keep your fears out. Curiosity, on the other hand, is what stimulates exploration, builds enthusiasm. It is curiosity that asks: What is out there? And is it a better place than where I am now? Poke your head out of your shell and take a look around!

How many times will you let fear win? It's normal to feel uncomfortable about the unknown, but faith is the belief in that which is not seen. Where's your faith? There's a place in a challenge that's never seen until you have the strength, confidence, and faith to step out of the comfort zone!

I remember so vividly the first time I went to the high diving board at the community swimming pool. Although I'd been swimming for some time and had gone on the lower diving board to jump and dive countless times, there was something about the high diving board that kept the monster on my back. I knew the day was coming because I wanted to experience the feeling of just jumping from the high diving board. Diving was another world! On one occasion at the swimming pool, my big brother was there and asked if I was ready for the challenge. I said a positive, very optimistic "YES!" He walked with me to the high diving board and simply said, "DO IT NOW!" I began to climb the ladder to the top and my little heart was thumping louder and harder with each step I took.

When I got to the top, I paused for a moment, stepped onto the board, and walked to the end. I took one look and turned around! The monster was winning! I went back to the steps to come down, but all the other kids were there waiting to dive. My brother waited for me there, saying, "DO IT NOW, Gregory! Where's your FAITH?" So I went back to the end of the board and stood there for about thirty seconds. It felt like forever. I said to myself, "I can, I can." And I jumped. It wasn't very long after that experience that I took my first dive without my brother being there.

Are you on the high diving board of life? How many times are you going to climb the ladder and turn around? How many times are you going to let the fear monster win in the game of life? I've been there more times than you could ever imagine, from my childhood to the day I decided to write this book. I refuse to let the monster win. I choose **FAITH**, my closest friend!

How do you expect me to respect you
if you don't respect yourself?

Give respect to get respect.
Speak to others the way
you'd want them to speak to you.

Be patient with the old and the dependent,
for one day you will be old and dependent too!

When you think about it, no one is truly independent.
Your greatest contributions to life are also
the beginning of your greatest blessings.

Think about it?
GIVE RESPECT TO GET RESPECT!

Day 22 – Respect Yourself

"The best thing to give to your enemy is forgiveness; to yourself respect." Ben Franklin

Aretha Franklin made r-e-s-p-e-c-t an anthem for all of us! But for a long time, we lost sight of respect in this country. Respect for the President, Respect for the Flag, Respect for The Elderly, Respect for Teachers or others in authority, and just simple Respect for One Another. Are the concepts that I grew up with so archaic? When was the last time you saw a teenager today getting up and giving his or her seat to an elderly person?

There can be no real success without respect, especially without respect for those who came before you. We, as Americans of all colors and races, are only where we are today with the multitude of opportunities we have to be successful, because we stand on the shoulders of those who came before us. We trash their memories, their great sacrifices, and the things they built. We *disrespect* the very freedoms we have gained when we cannot show simple respect for one another.

Whatever happened to respect?
I look around and I see bullies rampant on school campuses nationwide. I live in Miami, and I see how our immigrants from Haiti and Cuba—people who just want to escape places of little hope, of little dignity, of little respect, are shown just as little when they reach our shores.

Whatever happened to respect?
Domestic violence is one of our country's leading causes of death! Physical and mental abuses are out of control. In politics and policy, lines are drawn, sides are taken, and there is no longer respect for the right to agree or to disagree. One human being just decides they are *right* and that gives them the *right* to take control of another's body, mind, and soul.

Whatever happened to respect?
For our planet? For our one and only precious Mother

Earth? How can an oil company be allowed to show such disrespect for the earth and its inhabitants that they punch a hole through her very heart, with no plan to stop the wound from bleeding?

We have lost the ability to respect each other and the world around us because we have lost the ability to respect ourselves. Without respect, we suffer not only personally but also as a society. But it can begin with one person. Respect begins with YOU. Show some respect to yourself and spread it around in your home, in your workplace, and at the local a grocery store! Start by giving some respect, and you will surely start to get some back tomorrow or the day after that or after that....

Don't be discouraged; keep giving. How long will it take until you are respected? It's never too late! Ask Nelson Mandela. How long did he wait? How much did he have to take?

**It's very easy to stray off the course
and get blurred vision.**

**Distractions are the obstacles that pull you away
from the sunshine of every day.**

**Reaction from your perception creates
the paradigm in your mind.**

What you see is what you get!!

**Focus on nothing but the positive and the good,
and then the vision is understood.**

**Don't let fear in!
That's when blurred negative vision wins!**

Stay Fired Up! Stay Focused!

Day 23 – Remain Focused

"Most people have no idea of the giant capacity we can immediately command when we focus all of our resources on mastering a single area of our lives." Tony Robbins

Do you know why most people do not achieve a goal? Most of the time it really isn't because the goal is too hard; it is because people have a hard time staying focused on that goal. That lack of focus creates seemingly insurmountable obstacles. Being able to stay focused means more than merely keeping "your eye on the prize." No matter how clear the finish line is, it is impossible to stay focused if we keep thinking about how far we still have to go before we reach that goal.

That is why one of the easiest ways not to lose focus on your ultimate goal is to break it down into smaller manageable amounts. As you accomplish each small piece of your goal, you will begin to see the jigsaw puzzle coming together and your goal coming into clearer focus. For example, if you always wanted to write a book, do not think about what a daunting task it is to write 200 or 300 pages, but just focus today or this week or even this month, on writing just one page. That one page will put you one page closer to your goal. Do you want to lose 50 pounds? That can seem almost impossible at the outset. Instead, set a small goal to lose just 10 pounds, and then another 10, and then another. Or if you want to run a marathon, don't focus on that last mile, instead focus on the first!

I didn't run my first marathon until I was 43. It wasn't until I decided to get fired up and focused, honor the commitment, and stop letting the fear of failure win, that I was able to start my training. I distinctly remember when I could barely run a mile. But, because I was determined to honor the commitment, I remained focused. One mile eventually became easy. Then five miles became easy until I was running 10k meets and continuing to increase the mileage. I'm now training for my next marathon—a 26.2-mile race.

Even as a professional musician, it was very easy for me to lose my focus and get blurred vision from negative perceptions. When I came to Miami to start my production company and work the nightclub scene, I faced elements of the business that didn't surface until I decided to become a bandleader and a lead vocalist. Racism in the south was a given, but for the most part remained a hush, hush subject. My first band was a seven-piece show and dance band. The majority of the players were black. Every time I went to a club to play, the manager always approached the white guitar player and just assumed *he* was the leader. I was pretty tolerant with this pattern initially, but the frequency of the occurrence blurred my vision. All I began to perceive was negative, negative, negative! The fear monster was winning! I actually wanted to quit the music business. After a year of this madness, a funny thing happened—I reduced my band size to five pieces. The female singer and I were the only Blacks. I went from struggling to get jobs to having a full year of contracts and a brand new BMW. When the band was reduced, I took on the challenge of becoming the prominent male vocalist.

Remember, I'm the leader, the bass guitar player, and the sound tech. I was not a singer! I struggled with musicians that couldn't sing until I took some vocal lessons and just said that I could do it. All I needed was the vote of confidence from my vocal coach. She simply said, "Gregory, stay focused and believe in yourself!" The rest is history! I'm still singing and performing over twenty years later.

I know there's something that you've wanted to get focused about that you're running from. You're just letting fear win. You've got blurred vision. Now is the time to get fired up and get focused! It's your time! What's your perception doing to the possibilities? They're just waiting for you to go the distance.

ARE YOU HAPPY. . .

. . . WITH WHO YOU ARE?

. . . WITH WHERE YOU ARE?

. . . WITH YOUR LIFE?

Are you looking for someone to make you happy
in your external world?

When you start to feel good about yourself
from the inside, you will find the place
where true happiness starts.

Take the time to ease your mind.
Relax and let go of the external madness.
It's a false equation! In other words,
it all becomes history quickly.

Reflections for Remediation, Retention, and Recall . . .

Day 24 – Choose To Be Happy

"There are two things to aim at in life; first to get what you want, and after that to enjoy it. Only the wisest of mankind has achieved the second."
Logan Pearsall Smith

Happiness can be an elusive thing. In fact, how does a person even gauge happiness? Certainly throughout our lives what we think will make us happy changes. At age six, probably all it took was a heavily frosted cupcake. As an adult, what is it? A great job, a wonderful relationship, an African Safari? Or is that confusing happiness with wants or desires? Our Founding Fathers knew that happiness was something we all wanted, but also realized that it was something to be sought after, but not necessarily obtained. So they guaranteed us the Right to the "Pursuit of Happiness" and not the right to happiness itself.

Most experts agree that happiness is much less about the things we do or the things we have or even our achievements and accomplishments, than it is about the choices we make. In fact, many believe that happiness itself is a choice. Abraham Lincoln once said, "Most people are about as happy as they make up their minds to be."

I remember that whenever a student would come to me about a conflict with a peer, I'd simply say: "They can't get in unless you let them!" The visitor at the door of your heart is not always a welcomed one, but they can only get under your skin if you let them. I've left myself open for pain or despair simply because I chose to let in an unwanted visitor in the form of a person, or action, or sequence of events.

The external world has many dimensions, and we're all vulnerable to them to some extent, but we always have choices to make. To those who disagree in light of the lack of control we have over outside horrible or tragic events in our personal lives or on the job, I confess that our lack of control is true. You cannot choose the circumstances of your life, but you can choose how to react to it or how to think about it, and that is where the choice to be happy or not comes in.

81

Doesn't it make a lot of sense to arm yourself with a positive attitude that every day is a new beginning? We need to take the time to take in the peace and quiet of the stillness and to be empowered from the inside. In quiet reflection, we can hear the internal positive voices and tap into the source of a constant flowing stream of positive I-can-win energy. You see, your perception is so powerful that it takes the picture, sends the message, and waits for your reaction. This is usually the case when things are not going the way we want them to. We engage in a horrible internal dialogue that drags us further into the dark room of despair.

I remember failing the State Teacher Certification Exam. I was so upset with the world. I scored a 293. All I needed was a 295! Just one more right answer! I lost it right there in the computer room when my score came up. The testing room monitor thought I was crazy. All I could think about was the bad, the negative score of 293! I fell very deeply into the dark room of despair. I wavered between questioning my ability to pass the test and wondering if someone was out to get me. You see, my perception was so badly blurred that all I could perceive was the negative from the external. My happiness was totally consumed by the dark cloud of negative thoughts. But when I realized I had made a great score and I was much closer to achieving my goal, the next level in life, my paradigm shifted in the right direction. The rest is history! That was in 1994! I'm happy with my life now!

So how can we choose to be happy? I'd say the first step is to find a way to control negativity. Follow the 80/20 rule; find those few simple somethings that make you happy and do those. Do not dwell on the past, or the future. And I like the particular sentiments in this ancient Chinese Proverb:

If you want happiness for an hour — take a nap.
If you want happiness for a day — go fishing.
If you want happiness for a year — inherit a fortune.
If you want happiness for a lifetime — help someone else.

No one has ever said that life is supposed to be easy.
So don't be so hard on yourself.

If a challenge in life seems to be too much to handle,
it's that way for a reason.

Experience is the road to growth.
Just remember there are no rules to what road
you choose, and you don't get a map
to show you which way to go.

But you've got to make decisions
based on your own personal life experiences.
All choices have consequences
that can impact our lives forever!

Reflections for Remediation, Retention, and Recall . . .

Day 25 – Face Your Challenges

The ultimate measure of a man is not where he stands in moments of comfort and convenience, but where he stands at times of challenge and controversy."
Martin Luther King, Jr.

One of the ways that our body's immune system is built up is by exposure to germs. Each time we are exposed, we gain antibodies that make it easier to fight off that disease the next time it rears its ugly head.

Challenges are a way to build up your emotional, spiritual and mental antibodies. If the Source allowed us to go through life without any struggles, we would be weak, soft, and ineffective. We would never gain strength, perseverance, or wisdom. We would remain grounded forever and never fly!

How many of life's experiences can you recall that weren't a challenge to your comfort zone? When things are easy and predictable, we just go with the flow. No need to stress. No need to pass a test. But when we need to step out of the box and deal with a test, it becomes hard to even find the time to rest. In the moments of the challenge we become more focused and monitor what's happening more closely. During those times, we grow in new ways.

When I decided to become a teacher, I knew that it wouldn't be easy. I had been out of college for over 15 years and working as a full-time musician, which had nothing to do with teaching. I was very reluctant to make the commitment because I knew that I would have to make school my ultimate priority, even if I was a new daddy and working five nights a week as an entertainer. I had to take my son to a sitter and practice with my band and find the time to study and still be my wife's man. Yes, it was an act that a lot of times I didn't get right. But who said it would be easy to earn a bigger paycheck and meet life's demands? Now that I look back and have the time to reflect, I'm glad I made a decision to step out of the box. Now I have the credentials to knock on the doors that could open opportunities that at one time in my life I would have never thought possible. If they made it easy to grow in life, no one would make the sacrifice. We'd all just stay in the box.

**It's far more important to have a high level of
Self esteem than it is to have a high I.Q.**

Love Yourself!

Love Life!

The world needs your contribution.

Unique is what you'll always be,

So don't be afraid to let your inner light shine brightly.

Day 26 – Love Who You Are

"You, yourself, as much as anybody in the entire universe, deserve your love and affection." - Buddha

Remember these familiar lines from Whitney Houston's Chart Topper ***The Greatest Love of All:***

"The greatest love of all is easy to achieve

Learning to love yourself it is the greatest love of all."

It is a beautiful and powerful song and a wonderful sentiment, but the truth is that most of us do not find self-love, or true self-esteem that easy to achieve at all. Loving and giving to others is a wonderful thing, and, as we have discussed in previous chapters, no road will ever lead to success without stopping to give help to others along the way. But we have all known truly beautiful, loving and giving people, who give so much to others that they have nothing left for themselves. A pitcher of water that constantly pours without replenishing will eventually run dry. We replenish the love and the energy we store to give to others, by giving to ourselves. This is not a selfish act. It is, in fact, how we can continue to give.

It's truly up to you! Being able to love yourself is your choice! Life may not always be fair, but that's not an excuse for you to not feel good about yourself. I know it's important for every student to make the best grades they can in school, and I'm sure every parent would love to see their kid go to college, but every kid in college doesn't have the IQ of a genius. Every student isn't college material. One thing that every student of life has to have, regardless of the level of IQ, is a high level of self-esteem. When you feel good about yourself, the universe brings you all the good you're seeking. It's just the opposite when you're feeling bad, negative, and predicting the worst that could happen. You can bank on it—the worst is just waiting to validate your negative thoughts. Our thoughts are just like wavelengths. We're all vibrating on different mental frequencies. How many times have you said to yourself, "I don't have a good vibe about something or someone?" You usually follow your instincts. How often have you ignored your gut instincts, only to wind up in a situation and saying, "I knew it!" That should tell you how powerful your inner voices can be! Take the time to stop and listen to them! Listening to your heart is part of loving yourself.

Loving yourself means changing the tenor of your inner dialogue too. Stop beating yourself up. Stop catching yourself doing something wrong, and saying "Gee, that was really dumb of me." Instead start catching yourself being right, and saying, "Wow, that was pretty bright of me!"

So how else can you love yourself? There are many, many ways. It starts with being good to yourself. You express self-love by taking care of your body, getting enough sleep, eating right, and exercising. If you look good, you feel good! Feeling good leads to self-esteem.

I start every day with meditation to empower my spirit with positive affirmations to keep my energy positive regardless of the negativity of those around me. I affirm that there is only absolute good in my world. Every encounter that alters that is just a false equation. It's their problem in their world. Think about it. Nothing is permanent unless you internalize and process it. Why not process only good thoughts? They make you feel good. Bad thoughts just make you feel bad. Good thoughts lead to high self-esteem! Bad thoughts lead to low and no self-esteem!

Case studies conducted on babies who were given nothing but loving and nurturing interactions by nurses and those who weren't nurtured and were rarely spoken to or given loving moments revealed that nearly all the nurtured babies cried a lot less, weren't sick, and almost always were smiling and active. The other babies cried constantly, had medical concerns, and didn't appear to be happy. If words can cut like a knife or be as soothing as a morning breeze even to an infant who just wants to be pleased, imagine what they do for us as adults in our times of need.

Self-esteem is priceless. It is developed from every encounter we have, good or bad, happy or sad. Take in the good and try your best to ignore the rest. Love yourself, replenish yourself. The more you do, the more you will find that you will be able to give to others and the more that others will want to give back to you!

Time and space will never erase
what life's experiences teach us.

To really enjoy all that life has to offer is
the only way to maximize every day.

Even when the days seem long and
things appear to have gone wrong,
there's always something good
to take from the experience
to make you strong.

So when the sun doesn't shine
and the rain starts to fall,
just remember to stay positive through it all.
The sun will shine again my friend!

Reflections for Remediation, Retention, and Recall . .

Day 27 – Take Control of Your Time and Space

"The only reason for time is so that everything doesn't happen at once." - Albert Einstein

Twenty-six days ago you made a conscious decision to stop waiting around for life *to* happen, and instead to try to make some changes to *make it* happen. You began to take control the moment you flipped open the cover of this book!

Today we are going to take a closer look at how to gain and maintain control of your lives. The number one principle of being in control is simple: Live in the Now. Too often we refuse to focus on this moment; and, instead, we let our minds wander, rehashing events from the past, or worrying about what may be in the future. Either thought pattern puts you right on the fence emotionally, spiritually, and mentally. With one foot in the past and one foot trying to reach into the future, you are stuck in the middle. Dwelling on the past and fretting over the future shuts the door on creative thinking. By understanding that each new moment is a uniquely fresh opportunity to start again from scratch, we can be anyone we want to be in that moment, go anywhere we want to go in that moment, unshackled by the past and unburdened by fears of the future.

I'm absolutely sure you can recall incidents from your past that have affected where you are in the present. We hear about traumatic incidents that become the heavy luggage of life's time and space from many people on talk shows, in magazines and newspaper articles, on the daily news, in movies, and in talks shared from public speakers. The reality is that our encounters do form indelible impressions from very early in our lives. Physical and mental abuse from parents or a spouse is very hard to erase. We don't forget, but we can and should reflect and grow. It's time to check that luggage. Take it out of your life. Time and space don't discriminate. Waste your time, waste your space. If you keep the luggage, it will only get even heavier and heavier along the way.

Every tick of the clock, every moment, is new, unconnected to the tick that preceded it. Each new second brings with it infinite possibilities. Your job is to keep your mind open so that you fail to see an opportunity.

No matter what has transpired before, the Source gives us 86,400 new chances, new possibilities every day. Embrace them!

Don't be time and space's next victim. Sometimes by not taking the time to live in the now and treasure each of life's precious moments we move so fast that the things that are really important in life seem to blur. Slow down, connect with your Source, and take the time to grow. . . emotionally, mentally and spiritually. Get the mix right. It's your time and space!

**When a marching band plays a song
all the parts are heard as one. Arrangement of notes creates
chords of harmony to be enjoyed by anyone.**

**Music is a universal language that any culture can
understand with their eyes and ears in any land.**

**Even if a musician cannot read, he can still hear the
harmony, indeed, and play a part that pleases.**

**A singer can find the part that needs to be sung
even if she can't see the harmony chord
that's written for everyone.**

**As long as there's an ear to listen and the right chord
is played the universal language of harmony is made.**

**We have the opportunity to live in complete harmony with
one another. Our universal chords
start with a smile rather than a frown
for both are acceptable by anyone that's around.**

**But when a chord has a bad note
the sound is not pleasing because,
like a frown, it's unwanted for a reason.**

**Try to keep harmony in your life by beginning each day
with a smile, the universal language understood by all
across the globe through every traveled mile!**

Day 28 – Find Your Lost Chord

"Life is a song - sing it. Life is a game - play it. Life is a challenge - meet it. Life is a dream - realize it. Life is a sacrifice - offer it. Life is love - enjoy it."
Sai Baba

There can be no denying music's power to change moods, particularly from a somber or angry one to a happier one.

From Gregorian Chants to Gospel music, there is a spiritual aspect to music that is undeniable. There is not a human culture in existence now or in antiquity that has not had music as part of religious ritual. There is even a belief that each of us has, or can find, our own "Power Song" that can help us to achieve all we want in life.

Music is, at its most basic essence, recorded emotion. When we listen to a piece of music, we share the artist's feelings on a visceral level. True, that can be sad, and who among us hasn't put on a painful love song to share in the misery after a bad break-up. But, by the same token, we can share in the elation of songs of joy and happiness, or any song or piece of music that reminds us of a particularly happy time in our past. We also have another very important life lesson to learn from music—the concept of Harmony.

When I was 16 my brother and I formed my first band. I was the bass player in a seven-piece band called the Mighty Good and Strong. We barely knew a handful of songs, but we knew when a harmony was wrong. When things are wrong musically, you just know it if you have ears. I had been in marching bands since I was 13. I played trumpet. We all were in our high school's band, so we had some training and decent ears. We were attempting to learn songs from the record to play in talent shows and in local nightclubs. We practiced almost every day after school in the band room. I vividly remember some of our biggest arguments occurring because of the vocal harmony or musical chords in the songs we were learning.

93

Remember, we were very young and no one person knew anything significantly better than the next guy. So we'd finally agree, even if it wasn't always the best harmony. But one day, while looking for amplifiers for our guitars and vocals, we met these two musicians who were twins. Their names were Richard, a guitarist, and Ralph, a keyboardist. They were our ages, but you'd think they were adult professionals. Boy, could they play! Richard could make a cheap guitar sound like a classic Fender Stratocaster used by Jimi Hendrix, one of the greatest rock guitar players of all time. The day we heard Richard play, we just smiled at each other and just knew there was harmony and musical chemistry. The universal language of the ears and eyes of music was connected. Richard came to a rehearsal and joined our band! Can you imagine a white guy playing with seven black kids in the 70s? This rarely happened. But we had innate harmony: we hit the right chord. After a few rehearsals we pleaded with Richard's parents to let them join us, and the next thing you know we were out performing everywhere.

The moral of this little story is very simple. Harmony can be found in anyone at anytime and anywhere. The question is: Are you open to let harmony in from an unexpected encounter like the one I had with Richard? If all I would have seen was a couple of white musicians who didn't look like me and who didn't even play the kind of music I played or listened to, I would have missed out on one of the greatest influences on my music because of ignorant racism. I learned so much in a short period of time from my harmonious relationship with Richard and that impact was everlasting, not only from a musical perspective but from a life perspective about people.

He was not only a good musician but he was a good person with a warm open spirit to share the universal language and harmony of the music. Remember the song, *Ebony and Ivory* from Paul McCartney and Michael Jackson? All I want you to recall is the line that said it all: "Ebony and Ivory, live together in perfect HARMONY." Just like the keys on a piano, maybe one day we all will live together in perfect harmony.

If you intend to win in life,
then you should be prepared to pay the price.

There is a sacrifice that's worth the price
when you look back at positive results
that makes you feel nice.

When life's challenges seems to keep you down,
and you can't seem to see the light at
the end of the tunnel, don't ever forget:
being a winner is one of life's toughest tests.

We're born with the innate ability to survive,
to win in life, not just exist.
Make the most of every day.
Begin with the attitude of a winner!

INTEND TO WIN!!

Reflections for Remediation, Retention, and Recall . . .

Day 29 – Never Look Back

"The best thing about the future is that it comes one day at a time." - Abraham Lincoln

Most people choose the easy route. Status quo, don't make waves, never put in extra hours by coming in early or staying late. They do not challenge themselves to be better, to do more. And that's okay; that is their life and their choice to make. But you, you have made a different choice. You have just spent almost an entire month on another path—a harder path to be sure, and one that ultimately will be more rewarding, for you, for your family, and for those around you. We both know 29 days of self-evaluation and change could not be done without sacrifice. I cannot know the individual sacrifices each of you who has come with me this far have already made, but I do know this—you have made them and will have to continue to make more to achieve your desires.

So how do you know if you have given up enough to achieve your dreams? Take stock. Let me ask you this: In the last months, how many times did you come in early or stay late, or otherwise go the extra mile to stand out from the crowd at work? How many hundreds of hours have you devoted on your own to learning new skills or gaining broader knowledge since graduating from college? Are you better off than you were ten years ago? Five years ago?

When you have a plan, a passion, or a purpose in life, in your mind, you intend to win! If it's success you're seeking, you'd better be prepared to pay a big price. You must decide—do you want security, which we have already pointed out is basically an illusion, or freedom? And if your choice is freedom, then you must go full speed ahead—and never look back!

Freedom is usually the result of a very heavy sacrifice to be in total control of your destiny and leave a lasting legacy for your family. I'm working on freedom. You see, you can always begin again. Even if, like me, you have had to return to the security area from time to time, that's okay. As long as you keep your intent to dive off the high board into the pool and swim for Freedom's gate again one day. Some of our greatest success stories have manifested themselves in a dramatic swim to freedom's gate.

I honestly started right off the high diving board as a young college graduate with a business degree. I was hungry to become an entrepreneur in the music industry. It wasn't until 15 years later that I decided to enter graduate school, leaving the quest for freedom, and sought stability for the sake of my younger son. I became a teacher for the security of a job. I don't regret the decision. My son became a gifted student, a good athlete, and socially adjusted with his peers. He is grounded with solid foundations for success physically, mentally and spiritually. Still, I feel the high diving board is waiting for me to take another dive.

Have you made sacrifices for family that seemed to stagnate your aspirations for freedom? Maybe you're thinking you're too old or you can't get the money for school. I could list many obvious obstacles that are simply roads to growth if you elect to take the dive from security to freedom. Freedom isn't for everyone. Security is a good thing. The foundation for any successful business is built on someone's dream becoming reality with a team of security-based employees who facilitate the freedom searcher's strategy for success.

Right now, innovative technology is running the world. Every day some new computer guru intends to win with a vision to be the new freedom giant on the tech block. They all usually start from the security block and the creative bug from the source shifts their paradigm to a vision of freedom. You wonder what would be the answer if you asked the CEO of Microsoft or Dell what they have always wanted: security or freedom? I'm certain of this, they INTEND TO WIN!

The power of commitment
makes all the difference between success and failure.

Focus fuels commitment's tank and the end result
is a deposit as real as cash flow in the bank.

Commitments are simply links
in the chain to the next level.

Before you can travel commitment's road, you must ask
yourself, "Do I have the map of my goal locked deep
in my soul where the compass of life
makes everything alright?"

Make the commitment.
More important: KEEP the commitment!

Reflections for Remediation, Retention, and Recall...

Day 30 – Commit to Your Future

"If I am not for myself, then who will be for me?
And if I am only for myself, then what am I?
And if not now, when?" - Rabbi Hillel

So here we are: Day 30. You are a time traveler; 30 days into your future—behold the new you!

OK, I realize that not all of you here and now on this 30th day will see and feel that they are a profoundly different person. In fact, I bet most of you may not feel all that different at all. That is okay because this book was designed to be 30 days to a BEGINNING, thirty days to break your old patterns of thinking and to bring you to a new place, where you realize that anything is possible.

The world is at a fundamental tipping point. Those who were once in last place are now moving out in front. Be part of that movement, be part of that light. The last 30 days have shown you how to eliminate the negativity that holds you back.

As the light grows stronger in each individual, so can it grow throughout the world. Make a commitment to be part of the light. The world needs your success! There is a transformation of consciousness that's taking place the world over. Your source has a plan for you here, and the entire world is waiting for your contribution. Commit to make a difference! No matter how many times you've taken a shot and failed. No matter how often you've been told by others, "No, you can't do it" or your own inner voice told you that you're not good enough, you have just spent 30 days learning one inescapable conclusion: **NOW IS _YOUR_ TIME!**

"To everything there is a season" and now is the time for people with greatness pounding in their hearts to fulfill their purposes. Now is the time for their great ideas to come to fruition. Now is the time for their talents and gifts to manifest in real and practical ways. It is time to shine greater and brighter than you have ever dreamed possible. Commit to the change!

We all know that commitment is easier said than done. Every obstacle you could imagine is just waiting to make the journey to greatness very difficult. Remember how important focus is to honor the commitment. Don't get blurred vision. When I made a commitment to become a cross-country coach for Flanagan High in September 1996, I honored the commitment for seven years. I also made a commitment to run at least one marathon a year as long as I was a coach. I'm training for my 14th marathon now. That's one a year for over a decade. That's commitment!

It was very difficult to honor my commitments to be a responsible father, husband, full-time teacher, coach, professional entertainer four nights a week, entrepreneur, and to train for the marathon! I'll be very honest here: I've always been a multi-tasker, but there were times when the walls were closing in from stress, but the exercise kept the stress down and I just loved what I was doing. I stopped coaching to focus more on becoming a speaker, author, and entrepreneur. Time management, diet, exercise, proper rest, spiritual empowerment from your source, and strategic goal setting are crucially important to successfully honor your commitments. Every one of your physical, mental, and spiritual obligations is an intricate link in your chain to successful commitment implementation.

It remains to be seen whether enough people using the techniques I have laid out over the last 30 days will truly make the world a better place, but I do know this, using this book as a guide will certainly make your place in the world a better one. And when you feel better about yourself—when you feel happier and healthier—you may treat the people around you just a bit nicer, perhaps with a little more kindness and respect. That will most certainly improve our world.

Personal Empowerment Recognition Program (PERP)

Questionnaire for the "New You"

Physically

- Are you exhibiting your optimum physical appearance (OPA)?
- Are you disciplined about exercise?
- What are you fueling your tank with?
- Are you aware of the consequences of ignoring the physical?

Mentally

- Are your goals set to achieve greatness with the skills you possess?
- Do you feel you're ready to meet the mental challenge?
- Will fear of failure be the winner?
- Are you a peak performer?
- Are you honestly trying to expand mentally?

Spiritually

- Are you in touch with the Source?
- Have you discovered where the real power is?
- Do you know how important creativity is to your success?
- Are you being unique or trying to blend in?
- Are you utilizing your inner perspective to grow from every external challenge?

On the next page, you'll find a Personal Empowerment Recognition Program (PERP) commitment pledge that will guide you through the next 30 days. Before you began the book and on the preceding page I asked you some very important questions about the three important areas of your life to establish a PERP for success.

NOW is the time to take action with your PERP. Make the commitment. Sign it. Copy it. Carry it with you as a reminder to remain FIRED UP and FOCUSED to honor your commitments! Good Luck! Remember to be true to the vision of releasing your INNER WINNER!

Personal Empowerment Recognition Program (PERP)
30 Days To a New You Commitment:

I _____ will remain FIRED UP and FOCUSED for the next 30 days on my Physical, Mental, and Spiritual commitments to establish my PERP for success in my life. I will affirm every day that I STRIVE to keep my commitment alive.

I am dedicated to a adapting a new lifestyle management process for SUCCESS.

Signed _____

Witnessed _____

Date _____

Get a witness that will be a positive reinforcement to honor your PERP commitment for the next 30 days. Have them call to help you stay fired up and focused, or even become a PERP partner with you. You want positive energy and lots of love! At the end of the month, assess your pre and post data. Make another 30-day commitment!

I'm going to be the first to say Congratulations! You made the commitment. Let the lifestyle change begin to become a permanent transformation. Call me if you need a coach! I'm ready to get you FIRED UP!

PRODUCTS AND SERVICES

Gregory "The Activator" Griffith
is available as a:

Keynote Speaker

Edu-tainment Specialist
The Activator is guaranteed to get your team FIRED UP!

Workshop Facilitator
Mind, Body and Spirit
Peak Performance Seminars
Time Management Seminars
30-Day Coaching/Training Services
Foundations For Healthy Living Seminars
Corporate and Individual Peak Performance Training/Consultation

We offer a free monthly E-newsletter
to keep you fired up and focused for success.
Please subscribe to the E-newsletter at:
www.theactivator.net

You can order any of the following services or products from our online store or call:
1-888-80ACTIV (22848)

Books
Group discounts available
30 Days to A New You
Activate or Stagnate

Audio CD's
30 Days To A New You
A to Z Strategies to Activate Your Inner Winner
(Free with a book Purchase)

DVD's
The 30 GG Factors
Get these personal empowerment tools **Free** with a book purchase!
Activate or Stagnate!
Genius/Greatness; Thoughts; The Contribution
The Fear Monster
Inspirational Strategies to kick and keep the monster off your back

Visit Gregory "The Activator" Griffith
on the social networks to get his latest blogs
and much more:

www.facebook.com/gregorygriffith

www.twitter.com/gregorygriffith

Ebooks and Audio books available

CONTACT INFORMATION

GREGORY GRIFFITH
30 DAYS TO A NEW YOU
PO BOX 824035
PEMBROKE PINES, FLORIDA 33082

1-888-80ACTIV (22848)
Fax: 954-435-4660
Cell: 305-498-2266

www.theactivator.net
info@theactivator.net
grif730@bellsouth.net

GREGORY GRIFFITH, CEO, CTM, M.S. Ed

Gregory Griffith is a noted and most sought-after Empowerment and Edutainment Specialist. Gregory has been a leader and motivator in personal empowerment for over 20 years as an Educator, seven-year Cross-Country Coach, Personal Manager and fifteen-time Marathon finisher. He created the Personal Empowerment Recognition Program (PERP) to help individuals establish physical, mental, and spiritual foundations to reach their full potential. Greg is a serial entrepreneur and serves as **CEO of the Omni Griff Corporation, Omni Griff Properties, and Gregory Griffith Productions**, a multi-media entertainment company where he manages to balance a very vigorous performance schedule for private corporate clients across the country. Greg also serves as Vice-President and Consultant for **The Urban Music Group**. He recently was inducted into the Registrar of **Who's Who in America** and is a member of **100 Black Men of America** and **Kappa Alpha Psi Fraternity**. Greg received his **BS Degree in Business Administration** from **Florida A&M University** and his **Masters Degree** in **Exceptional Student Education (ESE)** from **Barry University**. *30 Days To A New You* is the highly anticipated follow-up to his previous book *Activate or Stagnate*.